VISITORS'
GUIDE
TO
ANCIENT
FORESTS OF
WASHINGTON

Tim Crosby

VISITORS' GUIDE TO ANCIENT FORESTS OF WASHINGTON

by the Dittmar Family

for The Wilderness Society

with additional text by Charlie Raines

THE
MOUNTAINEERS

Published by
The Mountaineers
1001 SW Klickitat Way
Seattle, WA 98134

in association with
The Wilderness Society
900 17th Street NW
Washington, D.C. 20006

0 9 8 7 6
5 4 3 2 1

Published simultaneously in Canada by Douglas & McIntyre, Ltd., 1615 Venables Street, Vancouver, B.C. V5L 2H1

Published simultaneously in Great Britain by Cordee, 3a DeMontfort Street, Leicester, England, LE1 7HD

Manufactured in the United States of America

Cover design by Pat Lanfear and Helen Cherullo
Book design and layout by Julie Hoffman
Illustrations by Jon Gardescu
Illustrations on pp. 18 & 19 (repeated on pp. 41, 50, 51, 62, 64, 66) by Jenifer Rees
Maps by Kristy Welch
Cover photograph: *Hiker in old-growth Northwest forest* © Elizabeth Feryl, Environmental Images
Dedication: *Stan Dittmar* (photograph by Ann Dittmar)

Library of Congress Cataloging-in-Publication Data
    Visitors' guide to ancient forests of Washington / by the Dittmar family for the Wilderness Society with additional text by Charlie Raines.
        p.   cm.
    Rev. ed. of Visitors' guide to ancient forests of western Washington.
    Includes bibliographical references (p.).
    ISBN 0-89886-473-9
    1. Hiking—Washington (State)—Guidebooks. 2. Trails—Washington (State)—Guidebooks. 3. Washington (State)—Guidebooks. I. Raines, Charlie. II. Wilderness Society. III. Visitors' guide to ancient forests of western Washington
GV199.42.W2V57   1996
917.97—dc20   96-2700
                                                                         CIP

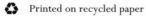

Printed on recycled paper

DEDICATION

Dedicated to the ancient trees that
have fallen and now nurture tall
seedlings, in the hope that the natural
cycle will be allowed to continue.

And to Stan Dittmar, who gave us so much
to live for and so many skills to live with.

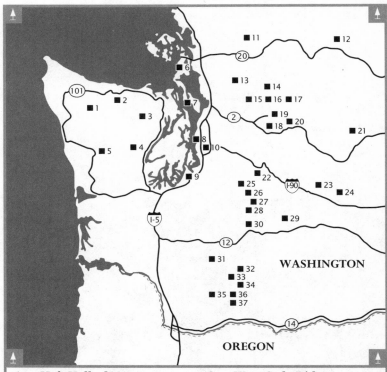

WASHINGTON

OREGON

1 — Hoh Hall of Moses
2 — West Elwa Trail
3 — Upper Dungeness
4 — Lena Lake
5 — Quinault Loop Trail
6 — Deception Pass State Park
7 — South Whidbey Island
       State Park
8 — Schmitz Park
9 — Point Defiance Park
10 — Seward Park
11 — East Bank
12 — Lost River
13 — Boulder River
14 — White Chuck Bench
15 — Youth on Age Nature Trail
16 — Mount Dickerman
17 — North Fork Sauk River Trail
18 — Troublesome Creek

19 — West Cady Ridge
20 — West Cady Creek
21 — North Fork Entiat River
22 — Asahel Curtis Nature Trail
23 — Silver Creek
24 — West Fork Teanaway River
25 — Federation Forest
26 — The Dalles Campground
27 — Snoquera Falls
28 — Skookum Flats
29 — Bumping Lake
30 — Grove of the Patriarchs
31 — Green River
32 — Upper Yellowjacket
33 — Upper Clear Creek
34 — Quartz Creek
35 — Cedar Flats
36 — Lewis River
37 — Big Hollow

CONTENTS

Peter Morrison

FOREWORD

After the last ice age the Pacific Northwest grew into endless forests of some of the world's most majestic trees. From time to time patches would be killed by windstorm, fire, or volcano, but vast stretches remained primeval forest. Coastal Northwest Indians traveled the waterways more than the land, because the tangled forest floor made passage difficult.

When pioneer settlers arrived, their first and most daunting task was clearing trees to conquer the wilderness. The hills of Seattle fed Henry Yesler's sawmill; Everett was founded by timber entrepreneurs; from harbors up and down the coast, pilings and lumber were shipped to San Francisco. The power of humans to transform the landscape is dramatically evidenced by the need, after only 150 years of settlement, for a guidebook to help people find any virgin forest at all in the Evergreen State. An initial glance at this book might lead one to think many examples survive of the original forest. Certainly the places described here have big trees. But fragments should not be confused with a forest. Groves near populated areas are few and small. In some places only remnant large trees stand amid younger forest. To reach intact stands of ancient forest can require miles of driving dirt roads, sometimes only to be blocked by a logging operation barring the way. Of the original forest that remains today, much may soon be gone.

Most ancient forest still standing is managed by the U.S. Forest Service and the National Park Service, and much of that controlled by the Forest Service is subject to logging. As can be seen most clearly from the air, Washington's canopy of forest is increasingly fragmented. If past patterns of timber sales and clearcuts continue, ancient forest may disappear except within official wilderness and parks. If that happens, the woods protected could be little more than tree museums.

All of us, indeed all the world, owe profound gratitude to the citizens and political leaders who protected forests in national, state, and local parks and in the National Wilderness Preservation System. A very few large sections of forest will remain, subject only to changes of nature. But even wilderness areas specifically established to protect

marvelous ancient forest, such as the Clearwater Wildernesses north of
Mount Rainier, may not include the best of the contiguous forest giants.
New steps must be taken to protect the ancient forest. We rightly decry
destruction of tropical rain forests, but to date only fifteen percent of
the Amazon basin is gone while over ninety percent of the old growth of
the Northwest has been cut.

The Wilderness Society has long led the charge for the great
forests of the Pacific Northwest. In 1936 its magazine championed "The
Third Greatest American Tree," the Douglas-fir of the Olympic Peninsula. The Society has published studies on Forest Service management
plans in the Northwest, on the region's timber economy, and on the
inventory of old growth actually remaining in national forests (see
"Suggested Reading"). Working with many others we hope to inform all
Americans of the plight of the Northwest's ancient forests. Working
with Congress and government agencies we citizens must end the
wholesale destruction of the magnificent heritage that is our ancient
forests. We ask your help.

—*Pacific Northwest Regional Office*
The Wilderness Society

INTRODUCTION

This visitors' guide to ancient forests in Washington State invites you to take a stroll through our Northwest heritage and gather a sense of life as it was before the Space Needle and ferry boats, before airplanes and loggers.

Using this guide you can seek out the past, take a hike into history, and pay your respects to the ancient forests. These few remaining stands were once part of one of the greatest natural ecosystems that ever evolved on our planet. Visit the old trees and come to an understanding of the complex yet delicate balance that has kept some of these giant trees alive for nearly a thousand years. In the ancient forest you can absorb the wisdom of the ages while being sheltered from the frenzy of modern life.

Once you are deep inside the forest, stop for a spell and touch the spongy mosses, peer into the logs' crevices, and smell the bark. Take a moment to sit and count the various shades of green and let the forest canopy shelter you from the sun or rain. Notice the crumbling log that gives life to the towering giants as well as the smallest of mushrooms and lichens. Let yourself relax, breathe into the deep earth and out into the sky, becoming a part of the forest.

Use this guidebook to launch your own adventure to some of the last fragments of old growth while these treasures are still standing. Now is the time to visit and enjoy their beauty.

What to Take: Before heading out into the woods, you should be prepared. The sites listed in this book vary from paved and well-signed nature trails to dirt roads, trails, and trackless backcountry. If you will be off the main-traveled ways, get a good map that shows all the roads and trails. You can get such maps from the Forest Service or from an outdoor sporting goods store.

Hikers should take the "Ten Essentials": extra clothing, extra food, a first-aid kit, firestarter (for wet wood), matches (in a waterproof container), a knife (for making kindling and for first aid), sunglasses, good maps, a compass, and a flashlight (with extra bulbs and batteries). For longer or overnight trips, take water, a filter or chemicals for purifying water, a watch, toilet paper, and an emergency signaling device (mirror, whistle, or brightly colored cloth or plastic). Nature can be unforgiving at times to people who are not properly prepared.

For travel in more remote areas, check the weather conditions before heading out. Call the ranger station; better yet, stop by on your way to the area (keeping in mind they may be closed on weekends). Forest and park staff are always happy to provide you with information and to tell you about the current trail conditions.

Most important, use your common sense. You are going on these trips to enjoy some of nature's oldest gifts. Spend the few minutes it takes to prepare before you reach your destination, so that you can give your full attention to the wonders of the woods.

What to Leave: Leave the forests just as they were when you entered them: natural and free of reminders of humans and civilization. Leave only footprints and take with you only the memories of the sights, sounds, and smells you experience in the wonderful world of ancient forests.

A NOTE ABOUT SAFETY

Safety is an important concern in all outdoor activities. No guidebook can alert you to every hazard or anticipate the limitations of every reader. Therefore, the descriptions of roads, trails, routes, and natural features in this book are not representations that a particular place or excursion will be safe for your party. When you follow any of the routes described in this book, you assume responsibility for your own safety. Under normal conditions, such excursions require the usual attention to traffic, road and trail conditions, weather, terrain, the capabilities of your party, and other factors. Because many of the lands in this book are subject to development and/or change of ownership, conditions may have changed since this book was written that make your use of some of these routes unwise. Always check for current conditions, obey posted private property signs, and avoid confrontations with property owners or managers. Keeping informed on current conditions and exercising common sense are the keys to a safe, enjoyable outing.

—*The Mountaineers*

WHAT IS AN OLD-GROWTH FOREST?

O ld growth is a technical term for ancient virgin forests. An old-growth forest is more than just big trees; many factors are included in official definitions. For simplicity's sake, the following is an overview of the characteristics that will help you identify the ancient forests in Washington.

An old-growth forest is a complex, diverse, and highly evolved ecosystem. The centerpiece of the system is the trees. Old-growth forests have never been logged and the dominant trees that are still standing and growing are at least 200 years old—some are even 1,000 years old. Many species and sizes of trees, some with broken tops, create uneven canopies, a multi-layered forest ceiling. Old-growth forests also have dead trees, still standing, that provide shelter for swifts and bats, and food for woodpeckers and lichens. And there are fallen giants, necessary to provide nutrients in the soil and to give life to seedlings which may someday become ancient trees. Also, old-growth forests have fallen trees in streams that give nutrients and energy to the waters, helping to support life from caddis flies to mighty salmon.

The lives of thousands of plants, animals, and insects revolve around the life-cycle of the old-growth trees. One life gives life to others—multiple layers each dependent upon the other as the chain of life weaves an intricate web of survival. From bacteria and fungus spores on and under the ground to the northern flying squirrel and the spotted owl high in the branches, each living thing relies on this complex balance.

How to Identify Common Conifers of Washington

These descriptions are only an introduction, to whet your appetite for tree books. Some incidental facts: Douglas-fir is not a fir tree, which explains the hyphen in its spelling; in fact, its scientific name means false hemlock. Similarly, redcedar and Alaska yellowcedar are not cedar to botanists. When needles come off true firs they leave a slight depression in the twig. Look below to see how Sitka spruce is different.

Pacific Silver Fir: *Abies amabilis*

Key Features. Bark is ghost gray with white splotches, almost always smooth; bud tips are purplish, spherical, and covered with resin. Needles grow perpendicular from the two sides of the twig but from the top lie parallel to it, pointing toward the end and concealing the twig.
Needles. ¾ to 1¼ inches long, dark green above with two bands of silvery white below. Needles are notched on the lower branches, pointed on the upper branches.
Cones. 3½ to 6 inches long, dark purple, sit upright in clusters on upper branches but disintegrate on tree.
Bark. Ghost gray with white splotches, smooth or finely grooved with resin blisters.

Douglas-fir: *Pseudotsuga menziesii*

Key Features. Cones have 3-pointed bracts between scales; branches end in sharp mahogany-colored tips.

Needles. Attached singly on all sides of stems, not patterned, flattened appearance, lemony smell.

Cones. 1¼ to 4¼ inches long, oval, brown, hang down, 3-pointed bracts between scales.

Bark. Mature trees have thick red-brown bark with very deep fissures; young trees have thin, grayish bark with sap blisters.

Western Hemlock: *Tsuga heterophylla*

Key Features. Top droops like a whip; quantities of tiny cones. Viewed from below the short needles give the canopy a lacy appearance.

Needles. ¼ to ¾ inch long, dark, glossy, yellow-green at tips of branches, single groove on top of each needle, blunt tip, two distinct lengths of needles in double file on twig.

Cones. ¾ to 1 inch long, oval, light brown, hang from branch, soft scales, very plentiful.

Bark. Deeply divided into broad, flat ridges covered by brown scales tinged with red. Young trees have thin, dark orange-brown bark separated by shallow fissures into narrow flat plates.

Western Redcedar: *Thuja plicata*

Key Features. Has scales instead of needles for leaves; bark is stringy.
Leaves. ⅛ to ¼ inch long, scales grow in pairs on alternate sides of twigs. Shiny yellow-green with a resinous odor.
Cones. ½ inch long, light brown, 4-6 pairs of thin leathery scales. Cones sit erect but lean back toward the trunk.
Bark. Mostly cinnamon, older parts are gray-brown from weather, broken into long fibrous strands. Usually trunk is heavily buttressed.

Grand Fir: *Abies grandis*

Key Features. Needles are longer than any other conifer except pine.
Needles. 1 to 2¼ inches long, glossy, blunt tips. On bottom branches needles are two distinct lengths and are on two comblike rows pressed flat as if in a book.
Cones. 2 to 4 inches long, yellow-green or greenish-purple at maturity. Seldom seen because they stand erect on topmost branches and disintegrate on the tree.
Bark. Smooth ashy brown and blotchy when young. Tarred, horny, ashy gray with long, sharp ridges divided by shallow, narrow fissures when mature.

Noble Fir: *Abies procera*

Key Features. Trunk like a tall pillar before reaching branches. Viewed from below, the pattern of branches in the canopy is geometric, almost polygon-shaped.
Needles. Stiff, crowded, turn up on twig to resemble a brush, pale to bluish-green with two whitish lines both top and bottom.
Cones. 4½ to 7 inches long, 2½ inches thick. Barrel-like form with papery bracts bent down over cone scales. Stand on branches.
Bark. Ashy brown, ridged into long plates that flake off to show purplish tone under bark.

Sitka Spruce: *Picea sitchensis*

Key Features. Very sharp, stiff needles; bark is scaled. Trunk is a straight column above a slightly flared base.
Needles. ½ to 1 inch long all around twig; stiff, sharp-pointed, light yellow-green. When needles come off they leave a little peg on the branch.
Cones. 2 to 4 inches long, buff-colored, papery scales with scalloped ends. Hang at ends of branches.
Bark. Reddish-brown with rounded scales.

Ponderosa Pine: *Pinus ponderosa*

Key Features. Tall, straight trunk with slightly flared base. Long needles in bundles of 3; platy, orange bark.
Needles. 5 to 8 inches long, borne in bundles of three.
Cones. 3 to 5 inches long, egg-shaped with a sharp prickle on the back of each cone scale.
Bark. In old trees divided into distinct orange "plates." Dark brown and furrowed on young trees (less than 120 years). Occasionally vanilla-scented.

Western Larch: *Larix occidentalis*

Key Features. Deciduous conifer, needles turn color and drop in autumn. Needles in radiating clusters. Reddish, pillar-like trunk.
Needles. Soft, light green (in summer), grow in clusters on small woody lumps or "spur shoots." By October leaves turn yellowish, by November golden-yellow. No needles November to April.
Cones. 1 to 1½ inches long, papery. Small, pointed bracts stick out from between each scale.
Bark. Reddish, scaly, becoming furrowed and plated, very dense (6 inches thick at base of older trees).

Lodgepole Pine: *Pinus contorta*

Key Features. Straight, slender trunks; prolific cone bearer.

Needles. 2 inches long, borne in bundles of 2.

Cones. 1½ to 2 inches long, covered with prickles, remain on trees for decades, very plentiful. Cones are "serotinous": scales are sometimes sealed shut by resin, locking seeds inside that may be opened later by the heat of a fire.

Bark. Orange-brown to dark gray, scaly, ¼ inch thick.

Western White Pine: *Pinus monticola*

Key Features. Long, clear trunk and slender crown. Regularly spaced branches. Uppermost boughs stretch out and up. Thrives in poor (gravelly to boggy) soil.

Needles. 2 to 4 inches long, slender, flexible, whitish-blue, borne in bundles of 5.

Cones. 6 to 10 inches long, slender, very pitchy. Large cones dangle from branch tips of even young (15 years) trees and are bright green until felled.

Bark. On mature trees, bark is gray, thin and "checkered" or deeply cut into small, regular squares.

Tim Crosby

OLYMPIC PENINSULA

Nowhere else in Washington will you find the variety of landscapes and climate conditions that exist on the Olympic Peninsula. With its rugged mountains, ocean beaches, and dense rain forests, the Olympic Peninsula has areas of heavy rainfall—as much as 12 feet per year on the western side—as well as portions that are semiarid.

Local climates influence which types of trees dominate a forest. Douglas-fir grow mostly in the northern, eastern, and southern parts of the peninsula where the climate is drier than the western slopes. This species thrives in sunlight and is the most likely candidate to sprout up after a fire or windstorm. Western hemlock, our state tree, can grow almost anywhere and does well in shade. You will often find hemlock thriving in the shade of the Douglas-fir, and when a stand of Douglas-fir trees reaches the end of its life cycle, western hemlock emerge as the dominant species, creating what is called a climax forest.

Western redcedar are found in the wetter areas such as the river valleys and lowlands. Sitka spruce predominate on the western side of the Olympics where they thrive in the high rainfall and abundant fog from the ocean.

Lena Lake

Douglas-fir

Lena Lake is in the drier southeastern portion of the Olympics, only about a 3-hour drive from Seattle. The valley bottom was logged earlier in the century and much of the rest was decimated by fire, but the stands farther along the Lena Lake Trail are spectacular.

The popular trail starts out wide and easy as it slowly climbs the hillside leading through second-growth trees. It continues to climb gradually as the path narrows and enters magnificent virgin forest. Look for Douglas-fir up to 5 feet in diameter and western redcedar more than 6 feet thick. This eastern Olympic forest of Douglas-fir and western hemlock is quite different from the spruce/hemlock forests of the wet west side of the peninsula. In spring, rhododendrons in bloom delight the eye.

After about 3 miles of steady rise the trail arrives at Lena Lake. The cliffs above look down on the lake surrounded by virgin forest. An excellent campsite in the midst of old growth is at the lake's north end.

The future of these trees is in question. Although there are no immediate logging plans, this could change, as the area is not protected. Conservationists had hoped that eventually Congress would safeguard the lake and surrounding forest by designating it as wilderness—no trees can be cut in a congressionally designated wilderness area. However, the Forest Service has allowed mountain bikes around Lena Lake, which will make it more difficult for the area to receive wilderness designation.

⚲ *Getting There:* From Highway 101 turn east onto the Hamma Hamma River Road (Forest Service Road 25) north of Eldon. The Lena Lake trailhead, almost 10 miles after the turnoff, is on the right-hand side of the road. No motorized use of the trail is allowed. Contact the Quilcene Ranger Station for more information.

deer mouse

Quinault Loop Trail

This network of three trails in Lake Quinault's south shore area leads you on educational walks through untouched ancient forests. The trails are well signed, acquainting you with some of their special features. Sitka spruce and western hemlock predominate in this area, but you will also see western redcedar, Douglas-fir, and bigleaf maple.

Each trail has its own highlights. Along the Quinault Loop Trail you encounter a swamp where cedar thrive. Down the Willaby Creek Trail, an unbelievably huge old cedar stands proud. The Rain Forest Trail exhibits a classic example of an ancient forest; some of the Douglas-firs along this trail are up to 8 feet in diameter and nearly 500 years old. All three of these hikes are easy, but don't hurry—allow a few hours to truly enjoy all they have to offer.

This is one of the most impressive stands of old-growth forest in the state. Watch for eagles, blue herons, and little songbirds. Perhaps you will see an osprey nest. In winter look for elk. The forest floor is lush, with club mosses, ferns, liverworts—myriad plants to entrance the botanist or the artist's eye. Cascara trees, such as those found here, are stripped by local people who sell bark to laxative manufacturers.

We have Franklin D. Roosevelt to thank for protection of the Quinault Valley. After staying at the Quinault Lodge in 1937, he recommended that much of the north shore of Lake Quinault be included in Olympic National Park. Unfortunately, the equally majestic south shore was excluded, although the Forest Service has allocated it to dispersed recreation.

⚓ *Getting There:* Turn east off Highway 101 onto the South Shore Road (just south of Amanda Park). Turn right into the parking lot where the sign says "Quinault Nature Trail." Signs in the parking lot indicate the lay of the land and a map of the trails. Contact the Quinault Ranger Station for more information.

fisher

Hoh Hall of Mosses

If you have never seen a rain forest, take time to visit the Hoh Valley, especially the prime example of old-growth rain forest called the Hall of Mosses. Club moss, lichens, and licorice fern adorn the trees, adding ever more hues to the greens of the forest. The Hall of Mosses Trail is very easy, with only one small hill leading up to the 0.75-mile loop trail. You will see Sitka spruce—the dominant species in the rainy, cool, coastal fog belt from Washington to Alaska—along with western hemlock, Douglas-fir, western redcedar, and maple trees. Sitka spruce trunks are straight columns of nearly the same diameter all the way up, with bark in rounded scales. Most dramatic are the old-growth bigleaf maple trees festooned with clinging mosses. The ground is carpeted with emerald

Elliott Norse

Elliott Norse

23

leaves that look like huge Irish shamrocks; actually they are oxalis.

Be sure to stop at the visitor information center. Inside you can find out more about the native plants, animals, and trees. Other trails that begin and end there give you a chance to explore the different stages of forests as they evolve in the Hoh River Valley. In the fall brilliant yellow maple leaves contrast with deep green-needled branches. If you have time, hike for miles up the Hoh Trail that eventually climbs to the glaciers of Mount Olympus.

A couple of points of interest on the drive up the Hoh River Road: Don't miss the huge Sitka spruce tree on the right side of the road (there is a turnout and a sign). It is reportedly one of the largest in the United States. Notice the dead trees and logs in the Hoh River. These eventually will be washed out to the ocean, then battered back to shore to become some of the driftwood logs you find decorating ocean beaches.

⚐ *Getting There:* From Highway 101 turn east on the Hoh River Road (south of Forks and north of Kalaloch). Follow the road for 18 miles, past many clearcuts and the entrance to the Olympic National Park, to its end in the parking lot. Contact the Olympic National Park for more information.

West Elwha Trail

Nestled in the transition zone between the wet and drier sides of the Olympic Peninsula, the Elwha River Valley is a mix of virgin forest and second growth. Here, the climate is drier than the coast, but not as dry as the eastern slopes. Douglas-fir, true firs, and hemlock thrive here, but spruce do not.

Douglas-fir cone

The Elwha River, flowing from deep within Olympic National Park, once was home to a race of hundred-pound Chinook salmon still remembered by oldsters. Salmon migration, blocked since early in the century by dams, may be restored if conservationists prevail. President Clinton has made removing the Elwha dams an environmental priority of his administration. Removing the dams, which are located just outside the park boundaries, would open up miles of pristine salmon habitat in the park and bring back the historic runs that the dams destroyed.

Resident fish and the pretty setting make the river an attraction. Most people don't think of fish as part of a forest ecosystem, but they are. The Elwha's giant salmon attracted hordes of bears and eagles which hauled fish from the water. Fish scraps were snapped up by the other foragers and eventually became fish fertilizer enriching the forest soil.

The West Elwha Trail loosely parallels the Elwha River. About a mile in, the trail descends to a flat area where a few old trees remain. The other giants were cut down years ago by early loggers, before the park was established. The trail continues to the park boundary where the old growth stops.

Look for the horizontal slits—"springboard cuts"—in the old stumps. In the days before chain saws, loggers made these cuts into which they inserted springboards to stand on to get in better position to saw down the huge trees. Standing several feet above the ground seems precarious to us, but it was easier than the alternative: pushing and pulling a crosscut saw through the flared or swollen base of a tree.

⚑ *Getting There:* Turn south onto Elwha Valley Road from Highway 101 (west of Port Angeles). The road follows the Elwha River and, after about 4 miles, enters the Olympic National Park. After the ranger station, turn right onto Boulder Creek Road and cross the river to Altaire Campground. Park in any road turnout nearby if the campground is full. The trailhead is in the campground. Contact the Olympic National Park for more information.

golden-mantled
ground squirrel

Upper Dungeness

Located on the northeastern "rainshadow" side of the Olympics, the Upper Dungeness area gets only 20 inches of rain per year. The trail passes large Douglas-firs in a forest periodically thinned by fire and then rises to dry, higher country that resembles eastern Washington forests, with lodgepole pine and Rocky Mountain juniper.

The first 3 miles of the Upper Dungeness trail takes you through ancient Douglas-fir forest as it parallels the pristine Dungeness River. At the start of the trail the hill slopes up beside you to allow easy viewing of native plants on a "bench" of nature's garden. The first mile of forest, which has the nicest old growth, is not offically protected, but its proximity to a wilderness area makes it unlikely the Forest Service will log there.

David Dittmar

After 1 mile on the trail, you arrive at the confluence of Royal Creek and the Dungeness River. Just beyond, the trail enters the Buckhorn Wilderness. From this point on, the old-growth trees are protected by the wilderness designation and will never be logged.

The largest trees continue for another 2 miles on the trail. Some old trees have charred bark, evidence of past wildfires they have survived. The Upper Dungeness was one of the few areas never covered by ice age glaciers, and hosts many botanically unusual plants. Plants whose closest relatives may be hundreds of miles away were able to survive here.

The trail is easy and fairly level for the first 2.5 miles. Beyond, it climbs a hill to reach Camp Handy (a good place to turn around). Backpackers can hike on for miles into Olympic National Park or loop around to the Tubal Cain Trail.

The area is snowbound in the late fall, winter, and early spring because of its higher elevation (2,500 feet). Check with the Quilcene Ranger Station.

▲ *Getting There:* From Highway 101 turn south on Palo Alto Road
(1.5 miles west of Sequim Bay State Park). Drive about 8 miles to the
junction with Forest Service Road (FS) 28, and bear left at the fork onto
FS 28. Follow signs from here. Veer right at the sign to East Crossing
Campground (FS 2860). The road crosses the Dungeness River about 20
miles from Highway 101. A large parking lot is on the right and the
trailhead is on the west side of the river near the bridge.

Don't let these directions scare you—the roads are well marked.
You can get a good map that shows Forest Service roads from the ranger
station or an outdoor sporting goods store.

Ann Dittmar

NORTHERN CASCADES

W ith rugged mountains and many active glaciers, high alpine rivers and lakes, a national park, and several wilderness areas, the northern Cascade Mountains supply plenty of recreational opportunities. Ample rainfall makes this area more like the Olympic rain forest than any other mountainous area of Washington State. Many of its ancient forest sites have been subject to chain saws, but here are a few samples of stands remaining from the distant past.

grand fir

East Bank

When Mount Baker was active in the 1840s, embers from the volcano's lava ignited fires which destroyed some of the virgin forest. Mud flows also contributed to the destruction. Trees that survived these and later fires still bear the scars as proof of their battle with the flames. You will also see charred "chimneys," the outer rims of snags whose rotting cores were burned out. Baker Lake is a popular recreational area offering many scenic views and hikes, a small resort, hot springs, camping, boating, and more.

The East Bank Trail (#610), with fern grotto after fern grotto, follows the Baker Lake shoreline through some of the once-burned area. The hanging growth of vines, moss, and ferns, and the abundant new growth in standing snags and downed logs, are excellent examples of the forest life cycle. Woodpecker holes and shelf fungus on a bark-covered trunk help you notice that the tree is dead, but hosts other life.

The 4-mile trail is flat and easy, making it ideal for children. They will enjoy the puncheon bridge over a bubbling stream. The trail is good early and late in the year because its low elevation generally keeps it free of snow. Yellow violets, trillium, or berries can be found in season. Camp or picnic at Anderson Creek or Maple Grove.

This trail can be reached by boat. The Forest Service intends eventually to extend it the full length of the eastern side of the lake to connect it with the Baker River Trail. The bridge over the Baker River should be completed by the summer of 1997. The old Baker River Trail is in the low elevation edge of old-growth forest that extends through privately owned land, up the Baker River, and up to Noisy-Diobsud Wilderness and North Cascades National Park. There are huge trees in the Lower Noisy Creek Valley. This land was purchased by the government with money from the federal Land and Water Conservation Fund.

Though you are unlikely to see them, spotted owls live nearby, and even grizzly bears may wander the farther reaches of the forest. Look for waterfowl on the lake.

This part of the forest will probably not be logged right away, but there is the possibility of timber sales within a few years that could impact the trail.

🐾 *Getting There:* From I-5 head east on Highway 20 to the Baker Lake Road (just west of Concrete). Head north on Baker Lake Road, along Grandy Creek and to Baker Dam/Kulshan Campground Road. Turn right and cross the Upper Baker Dam. Continue 0.4 mile to the Y in the road and turn left. The East Bank trailhead is marked by a small sign 0.7 mile further. Contact the Mount Baker Ranger Station for more information.

MOUNTAIN LOOP

You may already have traveled the Mountain Loop Highway marveling at the great views and the vivid fall colors, but the old-growth forests easily accessed from the highway offer an excellent reason for a return visit.

The Mountain Loop Highway starts in Darrington on Forest Service Road 20, heads south to Barlow Pass and then east on Highway 92 to Verlot. Paved part way, most of it is a good gravel road. The portion south of Darrington to Silverton is snowbound in winter and the highway is often not plowed. There are too many hikes for one day, so pick a couple and come back to enjoy the others another time. Or stay awhile at a motel or campground.

A stop at the Darrington Ranger Station will give you good information about forests in the area. While at the ranger station, take a minute outside to visit the cross section of a 700-year-old Douglas-fir. In the year 1274 the tree was only 4 feet tall. By the time the tree died in a slash burn in 1971, it had grown to a whopping 9 feet in diameter.

*marbled
murrelet*

Boulder River

The Boulder River Trail, between Arlington and Darrington, west of the mountain loop, is a beautiful walk
through a thick, old-growth forest in a lowland river
valley. Abundant and exquisite mosses and ferns create a
junglelike atmosphere in some spots. The sights you see
along the upper portion of the trail are like what the first settlers in the
area found. Now lowland virgin forests are very rare; over the years
logging has wiped out almost all low-elevation old growth.

At first, the Boulder River Trail (#734) follows an old railroad
logging grade until it reaches the virgin forest with trees up to 750
years old. After about a mile you come to the first of several breathtak-
ing waterfalls. Water crashes down the 200-foot canyon wall into the
aptly named Boulder River below. Here the canyon narrows as you
enter the dense climax forest. More waterfalls pour down from the
walls as you continue up to Boulder Ford Camp, which is a campsite
and the trail's end. The well-maintained trail is 4 miles long.

The best times to see the waterfalls are spring and early summer
when the snowmelt sends more water down the river. The hike is also a
good bet in late fall when higher-elevation hikes are covered with snow.

In the river are small rainbow trout. Land animals are more likely
to be identified by tracks than by actual sightings. Look for signs of
cougar, bobcat, and black bear. At one time the steepness of the canyon

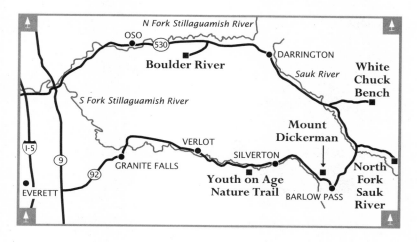

walls protected the trees from logging, because it was too difficult to build access roads. Since 1984 the area has been protected as part of the Boulder River Wilderness.

⚑ *Getting There:* From I-5 go east on Highway 530 through the town of Oso. Turn south on French Creek Road (Forest Service Road 2010) about 8 miles east of Oso, at mile marker 41. Drive almost 4 miles to where the road switchbacks sharply uphill and park there. The trailhead is at the end of the road.

western
hemlock
cone

White Chuck Bench Trail

Giant redcedar trees and river and mountain views highlight this primitive but easily followed trail, which generally follows the north bank of the White Chuck River. Douglas-fir, western hemlock, and western redcedar are plentiful. When hiked east to west, the ancient trees are along the first 3 miles of the 7-mile trail. You will likely see beaver ponds on this hike.

On the drive into the area notice the landscape scarred by clearcutting. These clearcuts are in sharp contrast to the undisturbed area surrounding the trail.

Conservationists have been trying to protect the White Chuck and surrounding lowland virgin forests since 1927. Their efforts resulted in the creation of the North Cascades National Park and the Glacier Peak Wilderness, but they have not yet succeeded for this valley. Most of the White Chuck's forest remains unprotected. The Forest Service proposes to eventually allow the clearcutting of more than half the area upstream from this trail.

⚑ *Getting There:* Follow the Mountain Loop Highway (Forest Service Road [FS] 20) south from Darrington about 10 miles to the junction of FS 23. Turn east and drive about 6 miles to the bridge that crosses the White Chuck River. Cross the bridge and turn left into the parking area. The sign for the trailhead is on the north side of the parking area.

western
redcedar

North Fork Sauk River Trail

The trail starts out in a lush rain forest of Douglas-fir with massive old western redcedars up to 9 feet in diameter. Feast your eyes on the awesome trees and rich undergrowth.

Giant trees line the first mile of the trail, but the biggest ones are found in the first 0.25 mile where the forest is unprotected. After 0.5 mile the trail enters the Glacier Peak Wilderness where, thanks to Congress, the trees are protected from logging. Beyond the first mile the trail passes through a marvelous cedar forest and occasional avalanche swaths. Follow the trail for nearly 5 miles through grove after grove of cedar, hemlock, and Pacific silver fir.

For the more adventuresome: After these 5 miles, the trail leaves the river and begins to climb. It winds through a series of switchbacks taking you higher and higher to sweeping views, eventually joining the Pacific Crest Trail near the 6,000-foot-high White Pass.

The North Fork Sauk River and Sloan Creek are sandwiched between the Glacier Peak and Henry M. Jackson Wilderness areas. As they did with the White Chuck Valley, conservationists urged Congress in vain that much more of this area be protected. The Forest Service has targeted much of the Sloan Creek drainage for clearcutting.

To see this threatened ancient forest, drive south on Forest Service Road (FS) 49 beyond the trailhead for several miles. Some of the trees have already been logged. Elsewhere, blue tags indicate the boundaries of future clearcuts. For splendid views of peaks in the Henry M. Jackson Wilderness, drive on to the end of the road.

⚑ *Getting There:* From Darrington drive south on FS 20 to the junction with FS 49 (about 17 miles). Take FS 49 east for 7 miles to the North Fork Sauk River Trail (Trail #649). The trailhead is on the east side of the road. There is plenty of parking in the Sloan Creek Campground.

Mount Dickerman

northern spotted owl

This is a steep trail with switchbacks that takes you up the side of Mount Dickerman, where your efforts are rewarded with spectacular panoramic views. Douglas-firs and western redcedars surround the trail as it ascends the mountain. The trail (#710) is 4 miles long, but you will find most of the tall older trees in the first mile or so.

The Mountaineers Forest Watch Committee reports that this trail could be impacted by the Stalwart Salvage sale, but the Forest Service does not think this will happen. Conservationists continue to monitor what happens here.

You may notice some newer trees growing among the old ones. A fire ran through much of the area in the early 1900s, and it was replanted in 1915.

As you ascend the mountain, take a look at the differences elevation makes in the landscape. The trees become smaller and the vegetation changes. Alaskan yellowcedar, found only at higher elevations, grows high on Mount Dickerman. You will also see spiky subalpine fir. Masses of wildflowers fill the mountain meadows after the snow melts; later in the season wonderful blueberries treat the hiker. This hike is strenuous, with steep switchbacks, so allow 8 or 9 hours for the round trip in addition to driving time. Bring plenty of water.

⚑ *Getting There:* From Darrington, drive south on Forest Service Road 20 for about 27 miles, and continue past Barlow Pass before heading west on Highway 92 (or drive east from Granite Falls on Highway 92). Watch for the Mount Dickerman trail sign on the north side of the road approximately 3 miles west of Barlow Pass.

coast mole

Youth on Age Nature Trail

This is a lovely, short walk on an easy, paved trail through old growth. The Douglas-firs along the trail are up to 500 years old, with the biggest just shy of 6 feet in diameter. Of particular note is an old Pacific silver fir more than 5 feet in diameter.

Along this self-guided nature trail are signs pointing out areas of interest. Be sure to pick up an informative map at the trailhead, the Verlot Public Service Center, or the Darrington Ranger Station.

On the trail are two fine examples of nurse logs. On one, western hemlocks get their start from nutrients in the fallen tree. The other log is quite a bit older—the roots of a large Sitka spruce and those of a western hemlock surround its remains. These examples show how fallen trees provide fertile ground and give life to the next generation.

The Youth on Age Nature Trail is a flat and easy 0.3 mile. The trail was paved by the Forest Service to make it accessible for wheelchairs.

This area averages more than 140 inches of rain during the year, so bring your rain gear! Due to the high rainfall you will see Sitka spruce here, an unusual sight in this part of the state. These trees are normally limited to the rainy Olympic Peninsula and wet coastline up to Alaska.

Youth on Age is another name for a plant you may have in your home—*Tolmica Menziesii*—also known as "piggy back." It is the ground cover that abundantly carpets the area; thus the trail name Youth on Age.

⚑ ***Getting There:*** From Darrington go south on Forest Service Road 20 and over Barlow Pass. Head west on Highway 92 (or drive east on Highway 92 from Granite Falls). About 10 miles west of Barlow Pass (8.5 miles east of Verlot Service Center), turn at the Youth on Age sign.

SKYKOMISH

Much of the history of the Skykomish River area, as with all the Northern Cascades, comes from railroad pioneers who opened the way for the flood of settlers. Early parties of railroad surveyors searching for a route to bring the tracks westward ran into trouble in the North Fork Skykomish area. Troublesome Creek gets its name from the difficulties they had in establishing a suitable railroad grade east of this torrential stream.

West Cady Creek and West Cady Ridge Trail bear the name of the chief surveyor who had mapped a route along the North Fork of the Skykomish River. Ironically, Cady's route was never used. The rails were laid along the South Fork and went over Stevens Pass by way of a tunnel. Contact the Skykomish Ranger District for more information on the three hikes described here.

Troublesome Creek

Tumbling Troublesome Creek cuts through a textbook old-growth grove. A 0.5-mile, well-maintained trail begins and ends in the Troublesome Creek Campground and follows both

sitka spruce cone

sides of the creek. Along the trail you will find a mix of young, intermediate, and old-growth trees. Miners who worked gold, silver, and copper claims as far as 2 miles upstream were the original users of the Troublesome Creek Trail. The trail ends at the upper bridge, but a faint old miners' trail continues north for another 1.5 miles on the west side.

High winds have felled many trees on the western edge of the grove. Some of the windfalls are close to the trail, which allows you to inspect their root systems. Roots of the Northwest's giant conifers are frequently shallow. They function well in gathering nutrients from the rich upper soil layer, but as you can see, they may not protect the

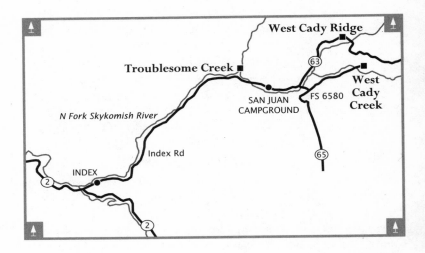

trees from blowing over in the high winds of a winter storm.

Notice the unusual deep blue-green color of the creek. The color comes from the minerals in the rocks that have dissolved in the water.

⬧ *Getting There:* Turn off Highway 2 (Stevens Pass Highway) onto Index Road and drive 11.5 miles northeast to Troublesome Creek Campground. Start your hike from either side of the creek.

West Cady Creek

The big trees on West Cady Creek stand in an unprotected but wild area untouched by roads, improved trails, or other signs of humans. This extensive stand of trees provides an opportunity to wander alone through an undisturbed ancient forest along a roaring creek. Many old-growth connoisseurs consider the West Cady Creek area a superior example of an ancient forest.

western hemlock

Huge Douglas-firs up to 5 feet in diameter and more than 200 feet tall line the undeveloped trail, along with western redcedar, western hemlock, and Pacific silver fir.

⬧ *Getting There:* From Highway 2 turn onto Index Road. Drive past Troublesome Creek Campground (notice the old growth on either side of the road as you pass the campground) and San Juan Campground. At 14.5 miles from Highway 2 the paved portion of the road ends. You will reach a junction 0.7 mile farther. Take the right fork, following Forest Service

Road (FS) 65. Turn left onto FS 6580. The road climbs through clearcuts, and at 3 miles you see a giant Douglas-fir over 6 feet in diameter. This behemoth marks the start of a strip of old growth along West Cady Creek. Drive 0.5 mile past the big Douglas-fir to the road's end.

Park at the end of the road, cross over the small brook, and go about 300 feet to where the trail drops down to the right toward the creek. Follow the bulldozer trail along the lower edge of the clearcut almost to the end of the clearcut to a slash pile. Follow the faint trail into the cathedral-like forest. The trail may be difficult to follow from this point on, but the open terrain and the roaring creek make direction-finding possible. Take along a compass and a good map.

West Cady Ridge

Roosevelt elk

The West Cady Ridge Trail (#1054) takes you vertically through an upper-elevation stand of ancient trees outside the Henry M. Jackson Wilderness. As you climb up the ridge, the species and mix of trees change with the elevation.

Cross the thundering gorge of North Fork Skykomish River on the footbridge and, after nearly a mile, start climbing switchbacks. The Sierra Club and a horse riding group have "adopted" this trail, so it is in excellent condition all the way to the top. At lower elevations, dens of devil's club and shoals of skunk cabbage line the hollows of minor drainages along with huckleberry, ferns, moss, and lichens. Elk tracks may be visible in wet spots on the trail.

On your way up the ridge, the trees become smaller and silver fir more dominant. Here and there, pockets of Douglas-fir and cedar giants grow in fertile patches of soil. After 3 steep miles, the trail reaches the ridge and follows it 5 more miles up through alpine vegetation to the Pacific Crest Trail. Along the way you enter the Henry M. Jackson Wilderness and are treated to spectacular views from Bench Mark Mountain.

Getting There: Turn off Highway 2 onto Index Road as it follows the North Fork of the Skykomish River. Go past Troublesome Creek and San Juan Campgrounds to the junction of Forest Service Roads (FS) 63 and 65. Turn left on FS 63, then drive 4.5 miles and cross the Quartz Creek bridge. After 200 feet you will find the trailhead on the south side of the road opposite the Quartz Creek trailhead.

Tim Crosby

CENTRAL CASCADES

🌲 FEDERATION FOREST STATE PARK 🌲 THE DALLES
CAMPGROUND 🌲 SNOQUERA FALLS 🌲 SKOOKUM FLATS
🌲 GROVE OF THE PATRIARCHS

Highway 410 along the White River is an often-traveled road, leading many Puget Sounders to Mount Rainier in search of scenery and recreation. Along the way are several sites within easy reach of the highway which contain some of the few remaining old-growth stands at lower elevations.

Ancient Douglas-fir, western redcedar, and western hemlock are the most typical old-growth species at low elevation in the Cascades. In autumn, alder and vine maple brilliantly color the hillsides.

Elk, deer, and bear frequent the area as they forage for food and drink from the White River.

noble
fir

Federation Forest State Park

Federation Forest State Park offers a perfect introduction to old growth and maintains a very informative interpretive center, open Wednesday through Sunday, April 15 to October 31. A network of well-marked trails includes two short loops. One is a little less than a mile long, the other about 0.5 mile.

Signs along the trails identify the many sights, and you can borrow a guidebook from the interpretive center for more detailed explanations.

If you must choose between the loops, pick the longer one to the west. The West Trail meanders through what is called "Land of the Giants," where you will come across some enormous old Douglas-fir and some of the largest western redcedar in the state. Ironically, the trees were saved from logging not because of their magnificence, but because they had center rot, a condition that makes them less valuable as timber.

Part of this trail connects with the historic Naches Trail, which ran between Walla Walla and Fort Steilacoom. Pioneers migrating west used this trail until 1884, when an easier route was cut through a lower pass in the Cascades. With the exception of the nearby highway and its occasional traffic noises, this forest is just what the pioneers encountered as they traveled toward Puget Sound.

Through the efforts of a group of tenacious women, this state park exists today. The Washington State Federation of Women's Clubs, in cooperation with the state legislature, opened Big Trees State Park west of Snoqualmie Pass in 1928. Wind, fire, and the axe were the demise of that park in the 1930s, but a new park—Federation Forest State Park—was opened on this site in its stead.

⚑ *Getting There:* Heading east on Highway 410, turn right at the Interpretive Center sign approximately 17 miles east of Enumclaw and park in the center's lot. The trails begin next to the center. Federation Forest is officially open from April 15 to October 31, but individuals can use the trails any time of year. Contact Federation Forest State Park for more information.

The Dalles Campground

Townsend chipmunk

Nestled among 300-year-old towering Douglas-fir trees is The Dalles Campground, a pretty spot where each campsite is sheltered by the sweeping branches of these giants. The campground's center attraction is an impressive 700-year-old Douglas-fir, so mammoth that, were it cut down, it would provide enough lumber for eight homes.

This tree is a survivor. It lived through a fire that swept through the area more than 300 years ago, killing all other trees. If you inspect the bark you will see the black scars that flames left behind. The tree was probably able to live through the inferno because of its age at the time. Older Douglas-fir trees have thick bark that insulates them against the intense heat of a forest fire.

⚑ *Getting There:* Turn right off Highway 410 at The Dalles Campground sign, approximately 26 miles east of Enumclaw. There is limited parking available for those who just want to see the oldest tree. The Dalles Campground is open from Memorial Day weekend through Labor Day weekend. Contact the White River Ranger District for more information.

CAMP SHEPPARD

Camp Sheppard, a Boy Scout Camp 28 miles east of Enumclaw, is the point from which the next two trails escort you through some magnificent stands of ancient forest and offer views of dramatic waterfalls.

The Boy Scout Camp area is open to all visitors, even when the camp is in session. The land is managed by the Forest Service, which means that it is yours to use, too. Contact the White River Ranger District for more information.

Snoquera Falls

western
larch

The Snoquera Falls Trail starts in Camp Sheppard. The trail originates in the parking lot and is marked by two parallel logs. Just past the trailhead you enter a Douglas-fir grove. Take a left turn at the trail junction and hike up the hill to the base of Snoquera Falls. As it climbs the hillside above Camp Sheppard, the Snoquera Falls Trail leads you through old-growth Douglas-fir trees, where moss blankets the ground.

This 1.75-mile trail takes you from 2,400 feet to about 3,100 feet in elevation. There are a few switchbacks along the way, making this a moderately strenuous hike.

The falls that await you at the high point in the trail are a spectacular sight in the spring, but the view is definitely well worth the hike any other time of the year. If you turn to look out over the White River Valley, you will enjoy another wonderful scenic vista.

Getting There: From Enumclaw, head southeast on Highway 410 for approximately 28 miles to Camp Sheppard. Turn left into the camp. There is plenty of parking available.

The camp is open year-round, but at times during the winter, snow may prohibit hiking. Make sure to check the snow levels before a wintertime visit to this site.

Skookum Flats

western
redcedar
cone

The Skookum Flats Trail is fairly flat and easy, leading you through beautiful old-growth Douglas-fir and western redcedar. Hike along the riverbank next to the lava cliff for about 2.25 miles. There you are treated to Skookum Falls and Skookum Seeps, where water seeps out of the moss-covered basalt cliff above.

Skookum Flats is across the highway from Camp Sheppard. The best place to park is in the Camp Sheppard lot. Then walk south along

Highway 410 to approximately 100 yards past milepost 53. Note the recent (1995) logging of ancient forest here to widen the road to highway standards. A small sign (6 feet down the bank from the road) marks the start of the trail that will take you to the Skookum Flats Trail. As a special treat along the way you will cross the White River via a cable-suspension bridge that was built by the Boy Scouts. Once over the bridge, follow the trail downstream.

⚑ *Getting There:* See the directions for Snoquera Falls. The Skookum Flats Trail is difficult, if not impossible, in the snow without the help of cross-country skis or snowshoes. Be sure to check the snow level before planning a trip during the winter. The elevation of the trail is 2,400 feet.

Tim Crosby

Vaux's
swift

Grove of the Patriarchs

This is a magnificent, virgin grove of western redcedar, western hemlock, and Douglas-fir on an island in the middle of the Ohanapecosh River in Mount Rainier National Park. If you are starting your journey from Seattle, it is quite a drive—about 3 hours each way.

The trees along this trail are huge and estimated to be almost a thousand years old. They have survived all these years largely because they are protected from fire by the river that surrounds the island.

The trail starts behind the rest rooms at the national park parking lot and leads you about 0.5 mile to a junction. Turn right at the junction and cross the suspension bridge spanning the Ohanapecosh River. Once on the island, the trail continues briefly before it forks. It is a loop, 1.5 miles in length, so you can go either way.

⬥ *Getting There:* Take Highway 410 south toward Mount Rainier to the junction with Highway 123. Take Highway 123 south, from Cayuse Pass. Turn right onto the Stevens Canyon Road past the park entrance. There is a parking lot about 0.25 mile from the highway and the trailhead is behind the rest rooms. Grove of the Patriarchs is open from mid-May to November. Contact Mount Rainier National Park for more information.

Bob Pearson

SOUTHERN CASCADES

🌲 BIG HOLLOW 🌲 CEDAR FLATS 🌲 LEWIS RIVER
🌲 QUARTZ CREEK 🌲 UPPER CLEAR CREEK 🌲 GREEN RIVER
🌲 UPPER YELLOWJACKET

T he Gifford Pinchot National Forest is a vast expanse of varied forest land. It covers 1.3 million acres stretching from Mount Rainier to the Columbia River and from Mount St. Helens to Mount Adams. The biggest tourist attraction in this area is Mount St. Helens; many visitors come to the southern part of the state to see the devastation that resulted from the volcano's 1980 eruption.

What these visitors may miss are the significant stands of old growth located in some lesser-known parts of Mount St. Helens National Volcanic Monument and the Gifford Pinchot National Forest.

The largest unprotected roadless area in western Washington (outside a designated wilderness area) is the Dark Divide. Three of the trips (Quartz Creek, Upper Clear Creek, and Upper Yellowjacket) described in this section are forests in or adjacent to the Dark Divide Roadless Area.

Big Hollow

noble fir cone

The largest unfragmented ancient forest between Lewis River and the Columbia River is Big Hollow in the Bourbon Roadless Area, located just east of Trapper Creek Wilderness. Douglas-fir, western hemlock, western redcedar, Pacific silver fir, noble fir, and western white pine are found in various parts of the Bourbon Roadless Area. Northern spotted owls live here. Lower reaches of three creeks host steelhead trout that migrate up Wind River from the Columbia. Big Hollow Trail is one of several trails in this rugged land.

Big Hollow Trail (#158) may be disrupted by clearcuts at its eastern trailhead. Leave a car here, if you can, but start your hike from the other end. Take Observation Trail (#132) south through old-growth silver fir in Sisters Rocks Research Natural Area. At the Research Natural Area boundary you reach open meadows and berry fields where a fire cleared

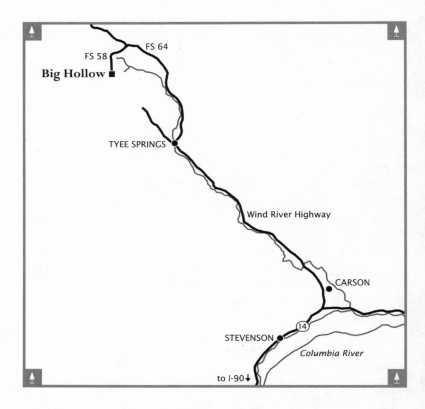

the forest in 1902. Western white pine adorn the slopes. Soon you reach
the junction with Big Hollow Trail and a campsite under the trees.

Hike down through natural second-growth forest regrowing after
the burn. It inherited the legacy of earlier old growth—the many huge
snags and downed logs provide wildlife habitat. As you descend, you
will find more and more large live trees until you are fully in old
growth. The steepness of the hillside allows you to see into the canopy
of ancient branches. After about 2 miles in ancient Douglas-fir forest,
you reach Big Hollow Creek. Ford the creek. You will get your feet wet,
but it is not far to the road.

↟ *Getting There:* Take I-5 to I-205 to Highway 14, which you follow
through Camas and Stevenson. Turn north on Wind River Highway
(which becomes Forest Service Road [FS] 30) and go approximately 13

miles toward Government Mineral Springs. At Tyee Springs turn right on FS 64. In about 4 miles at a hairpin turn, the eastern trailhead for Big Hollow Trail should still be visible. Continue on FS 64 to FS 58 to Sisters Rocks Research Natural Area and the north end of Observation Trail. Park by the roadside. Walk through the Research Natural Area to the junction with Big Hollow Trail and down the trail to FS 64. Get a good map before you head out. Contact the Gifford Pinchot National Forest for more information.

Cedar Flats

Discover the serenity of this ancient forest of western redcedar and Douglas-fir on an easy family hike. Cedar Flats Nature Trail is a 1-mile loop through a Research Natural Area, set aside to protect an area of old growth for study. Here scientists investigate many aspects of nature to gain insights into the wonders of this complex ecosystem.

northern goshawk

The stand is dominated by western redcedar nearly 200 feet tall. The dense, multilayered canopy screens out most of the light on the forest floor. The shade has thinned out the smaller trees and undergrowth, making it easy to see mosses, ferns, and other old-growth vegetation of the forest floor.

As you start your walk, look to the north to see an unfamiliar sight—a giant cedar snag whose broken crown provides fertile soil from which seedlings have sprouted. Along the way you will see more common examples of nurse logs on the ground passing their nutrients on to the next generation. Fallen trees lie at odd angles on the forest floor. When these trees fell, they ricocheted off neighboring trees.

Listen and watch for elk in the forest and down along the banks of the Muddy River.

Getting There: Take I-5 to Woodland (exit 21) and go east 29 miles on Highway 503 to Cougar. Beyond Cougar the road becomes Forest Service Road (FS) 90. Continue east toward the Pine Creek Information Center at the east end of Swift Reservoir. At the junction of FS 90 and FS 25, go straight on FS 25 for about 3.7 miles to the Cedar Flats Trail entrance on the right side of the road. Contact the Gifford Pinchot National Forest for more information.

*fringed
myotis*

Lewis River

A spectacular view of the Curly Creek waterfall as it spills into the Lewis River is at the beginning of a trail through a large ancient forest. Lewis River Trail (#31) plunges into a forest of aged Douglas-fir, western redcedar, and western hemlock. Some of the trees in this river valley are more than 500 years old; they would have been seedlings about the time Columbus sailed for the New World.

A fairly level trail as far as Bolt Shelter (about 2.5 miles) makes this an easy hike for all ages. Because of its low elevation, it is generally free of snow all year. Beyond Bolt Shelter the trail climbs up and down over rocky bluffs. The trail is 9.5 miles long, usually within sight or sound of the river. You will walk in old growth for about the first 4 miles. Beyond the point where Big Creek enters the Lewis River (on the opposite bank) the trail goes through natural forest that has regrown after a forest fire in about 1920. Take in at least the first 3 miles to experience some great examples of ancient trees. To hike the entire trail, leave one car at the west (downstream) trailhead and drive to the east (upstream) trailhead. The hike is best when heading downstream.

Getting There: Take I-5 to Woodland (exit 21) and go east 29 miles on Highway 503 to Cougar. Highway 503 becomes Forest Service Road (FS) 90, which goes east to the Pine Creek Information Center. Go

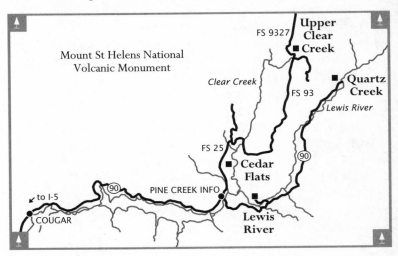

right on FS 90 at the junction of FS 90 and FS 25. FS 90 takes you through the hamlet of Eagles Cliff and along the Lewis River. At 5.2 miles turn left (northwest) on FS 9039, which takes you across the river. The trail starts by the bridge, but be sure to drive 0.25 mile farther to the Forest Service parking lot to see Curly Creek Falls. Contact the Gifford Pinchot National Forest for more information.

Quartz Creek

Pacific silver fir

Many creeks, lakes, and ridges in Washington bear the name "Quartz." There are two Quartz Creeks in old-growth stands in the Gifford Pinchot National Forest. The Quartz Creek described here is part of the Dark Divide Roadless Area. The other, near the north end of Mount St. Helens National Volcanic Monument, is listed in "More Ancient Forest Areas" in the back of this guidebook. Quartz Creek is a beautiful setting in an increasingly rare resource—low-elevation virgin forest. Many trees are 3 to 4 feet in diameter; some are bigger. The trail goes through two clearcuts already; this area is a prime candidate for future logging because its many large trees are easily accessible. The Forest Service has no current plans to sell this timber, but this could change and trees could be sold at any time.

The Mountaineers is working to get this area designated as wilderness. Motorcycle and off-road vehicle groups are pressuring the Forest Service to open the Dark Divide to motorized recreation, which would disrupt the roadless character and greatly reduce the chances it will ever be wilderness. A 1996 court decision acknowledged the negative impact of motorized vehicles in the area by restricting their use on certain trails. However, getting wilderness designation here is still an uphill battle for conservationists.

Quartz Creek Trail (#5) isn't easy. Platinum Creek is challenging to cross, and the trail goes up and down along the way although the net elevation gain is only a few hundred feet. For the best views of old growth, follow the trail up to the Snagtooth Creek crossing (about 4.5 miles), then head back. The best old growth starts just after the second clearcut (about 2.5 miles).

Look for evidence of deer, elk, and coyote on the trail. If you are very lucky you may see a flying squirrel.

🔺 **Getting There:** See the directions to Lewis River. Stay on Forest Service Road (FS) 90. The trailhead is about 17.5 miles from the junction of FS 90 and FS 25 and is just before the Quartz Creek bridge. Contact the Mount Adams Ranger District for more information.

pine
marten

Upper Clear Creek

Wright Meadow Trail (#80) takes you into Washington's longest continuous corridor (more than 10 miles long) of old-growth Douglas-fir outside Olympic National Park. Follow the trail about 1.5 miles to Clear Creek.
Here Elk Creek joins Clear Creek from the northwest in a magnificent canyon. A spectacular waterfall is just downstream on Clear Creek. To continue on the trail you must ford the creek, a difficult task unless the water is low. The trail now ends in a clearcut but may be rebuilt to connect with Forest Service Road 25. This is a somewhat strenuous hike that drops 1,300 feet to the creek, then climbs 800 feet from east to west.

For those experienced in off-trail hiking, Clear Creek offers one of the last opportunities to explore a forest relatively unimpaired by roads or logging. Use a map and compass to navigate. Look for impressive views of waterfalls and Clear Creek Canyon. Marvel at western redcedar and Douglas-fir averaging 6 feet in diameter.

Trout fishing in Clear Creek is superb thanks to the old-growth habitat. Log jams from the fallen giants and the woody debris make ideal locations for fish to feed and spawn.

🔺 **Getting There:** See the directions to Cedar Flats. Continue 1 mile, crossing the Muddy River. Forest Service Road (FS) 25 begins to climb steeply. At a sharp left curve, look for the junction with FS 93, and take that road. FS 93 takes you east and then north about 15 miles to FS 9327. Go to the left on FS 9327 and head north past Wright Meadow. At about 1.5 miles, look for the trailhead. Contact Mount St. Helens Ranger District for more information.

western
larch cone

Green River

Shielded from Mount St. Helens by high ridges, about two-thirds of the old-growth Douglas-fir in the Green River "Valley of the Giants" survived the 1980 eruption. The Forest Service reopened the reconstructed Green River

Trail (#213) in the summer of 1989. It is a 5-mile (one way) hike in a deep valley forest of trees more than 400 years old. As part of Mount St. Helens National Volcanic Monument this forest is permanently protected from logging.

Mines and miners' cabins dating back more than 60 years are located along the trail. The Minnie Lee cabin is an impressive structure built of massive logs, now gradually being recycled back into the forest. Watch for herds of elk in the valley, especially in the fall.

⚑ *Getting There:* Take Highway 12 to Randle; turn south on Cispus Road. Go 1 mile to a Y and take the right fork (straight ahead) which becomes Forest Service Road (FS) 25. About 10 miles from Randle take FS 26 as it forks right off FS 25. Go 12 miles and turn right onto FS 2612, which you follow to the trailhead. Contact Mount St. Helens Ranger District for more information.

Upper Yellowjacket

western white pine

A world-record noble fir stands proudly in a group of four noble firs in the vicinity of clearcuts. Noble firs are the biggest of the true fir species, and this is the largest known noble fir anywhere. It is more than 200 feet tall with a diameter of more than 6 feet. Although this current record-holder may lose some of its height because the top portion is dying, several candidates nearby are ready to take its place.

It is unusual to see such a concentration of oversized trees of this species. Moist rich soil at higher elevation combined with abundant sunlight created ideal growing conditions to produce the world-record and other large noble firs. Douglas-fir does not do as well in this moderately high elevation and gives way to the better suited noble fir. You can tell an old noble fir by its ashy brown bark divided by deep fissures into rectangular plates, and by its stiff, closely spaced needles that make each twig look like a brush.

There is no formal trail here (you should take along a map), but you can wander around the area surrounding the enormous tree and admire the other very old trees. Explore the Forest Service roads to the south. About 0.5 mile south of the largest fir the main road makes a sharp left, but an unmarked dirt road (Forest Service Road [FS] 051) continues south. Walk up this winding, unmaintained road. In about a

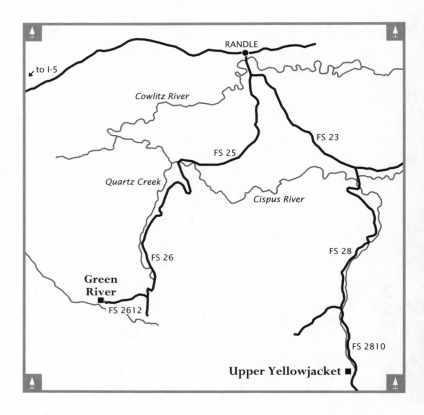

mile, after crossing three forks of Yellowjacket Creek, you enter still another stand of enormous noble firs. This exploration can be a good one-day outing, or it can be part of an extended trip on the Boundary Trail (#1).

⚘ *Getting There:* From I-5, take Highway 12 east to Randle. For road and trail information stop at the Randle Ranger Station at the east end of town. From Randle, take Cispus Road (FS Roads 23 and 25) 1 mile to the Y in the road. Take the left fork (east), follow FS 23 for 9 miles and then turn right on FS 28. The pavement ends beyond the bridge over Yellowjacket Creek, but stay on FS 28. After following Yellowjacket Creek for about 2 miles, watch for a towering 7-foot-diameter Douglas-fir as you pass below. You are likely to see deer here.

After 10 miles continue south on FS 2810 (don't take the main fork to the right). Drive 3.5 miles to a grassy, flat area with young alder trees. Across the stream, several hundred yards away and surrounded by a fence, stands the record-holding noble fir.

Tim Crosby

PUGET SOUND AREA

🌲 SCHMITZ PARK 🌲 SEWARD PARK 🌲 ASAHEL CURTIS NATURE
TRAIL 🌲 POINT DEFIANCE PARK 🌲 SOUTH WHIDBEY ISLAND
STATE PARK 🌲 DECEPTION PASS STATE PARK

O ld trees still stand near urban areas. Through the protection of city
and state parks, some of these ancient trees have been able to survive the growth of the cities; they serve as a reminder of what the
Puget Sound area was like before settlers came and changed the face of
the forest.

The old trees you will find in the parks are not, by definition, old-
growth forest. In most cases there are too few trees, not enough
wildlife, and a lack of the biological diversity you would find in a wild
forest. These groves are all that is left of the old growth that once
blanketed the area. But the trees are still big, very old, and impressive.
Consider these places an introduction to other more complete forests.

The sites in this section are close enough to the Everett–Seattle–
Tacoma area for an afternoon getaway or a picnic. Discover the ancient
wonders practically in these cities' backyards.

Schmitz Park

*grand fir
cone*

Who would believe there is an 8-foot-diameter Douglas-fir
still standing in West Seattle? There is, and it is a highlight
of Schmitz Park. A 0.5-mile loop trail escorts you through
the grove of huge Douglas-firs and western redcedar and
past a lovely gurgling stream fed by two tributaries. In this
microcosm of forest, all the characteristics that define old-
growth forest can be seen: large and small trees of numerous species,
large standing snags, big logs on the ground and in the stream. In the
core of the park the undergrowth is as luxuriant and diverse as in a
deep forest.

Most of the land that is now Schmitz Park was donated to the city
in 1908. The donors were Park Commissioner Ferdinand Schmitz and
his wife Emma. The couple wished to preserve some of the original
forest that greeted the first settlers.

⚑ **Getting There:** Head west on the West Seattle Bridge; exit onto Admiral Way. Stay on Admiral Way, go through the business district and then downhill toward the sound. The entrance is on the left just before the bridge over a ravine. Contact Outdoor Recreation Information in Seattle for more information.

fisher

Seward Park

Take a walk through a forest in the city. This trail through the giants takes you back in time, back to what Seattle was like before skyscrapers and hydroplanes. From the sights and sounds of the trail, you'd never know you were in the city (unless it's a busy summer weekend!). Even when Seward Park is crowded, few people walk on the trails through its woods.

Seward Park has been in the hands of the city for about a hundred years. Before the Lake Washington ship canal was built, Seward Park was an island. When the water level in Lake Washington was lowered, the connecting land was uncovered, making the island into a peninsula.

One of the tallest trees holds an eagle's nest; it can be seen from a parking lot off Lake Washington Boulevard but not from the ground below. Douglas-fir, western redcedar, and knobby old maples are survivors of the original forest, as are ferns, salal, and Oregon-grape. Try to ignore the weeds, but watch out for poison oak.

⚑ **Getting There:** Going south on Lake Washington Boulevard, south of I-90, turn left at the entrance to Seward Park. Park in the lot that is almost at the crest of the hill. The trailhead is across the road. Contact Outdoor Recreation Information in Seattle for more information. You can also take a Seattle city bus to Seward Park; call Seattle's Metro bus service for details.

pacific
silver fir
cone

Asahel Curtis Nature Trail

Unless you noticed the ragged and asymmetrical tops of the old-growth trees from I-90, you'd never know an old-growth forest existed in the median of the freeway. It has Douglas-fir, western hemlock, western redcedar, western white pine, Pacific silver fir, and noble fir—one of the last old-growth stands in the I-90 corridor. Some of these trees got their start in the thirteenth century and are more than 250 feet high; one is more than 19 feet in girth.

A relatively flat self-guided trail about a mile long leads you through the forest. Look for signs identifying various species of trees. Notice, as you walk, the dead snags and downed logs; these are necessary for the health of an old-growth forest. The decaying matter provides food, shelter, and nutrients for its inhabitants. The stand is fairly small, but if you could block out the freeway noise you might imagine yourself here decades ago with the naturalist and photographer for whom it is named, Asahel Curtis.

↟ *Getting There:* Heading west on I-90 from Seattle take exit 47 (Denny Creek/Asahel Curtis) and after exiting turn right; do not cross the freeway. Follow the signs for Asahel Curtis. At Forest Service Road 55, turn left and drive 0.5 mile to the end of the road and the parking lot for the trail. Contact Outdoor Recreation Information in Seattle for more information.

Point Defiance Park

*pileated
woodpecker*

Point Defiance Park is well known for its beautiful views, numerous activities, and beautifully maintained floral gardens. There is something for everyone here: a zoo, an aquarium, Fort Nisqually, a boathouse, beaches, trails, and roads winding through the whole park. There is even a replica of an old logging camp at Camp Six. Tacoma residents are justifiably proud of these special grounds.

What is not well known, however, is that there are Douglas-firs more than 7 feet in diameter here. One tree, the Mountaineer Tree, started growing about the time Shakespeare was born, in 1564. This giant is more than 200 feet tall.

The park is big—700 acres—and ranks as the twelfth-largest city park in the United States. The peninsula was used by the Hudson's Bay Company as a fur trading post in the mid-1800s. It was then used as a military reservation until the city of Tacoma obtained the land in 1905.

↟ *Getting There:* From I-5 take exit 132 (southwest of the Tacoma Dome) to Highway 16. Heading northeast take the 6th Avenue exit and turn left. Within one block turn right onto Pearl Street and drive directly into the park. Once in the park, follow the signs for Five Mile Drive. Many trails lead off Five Mile Drive; the old growth is throughout the northern end of the peninsula. Contact the Washington State Parks and Recreation Commission for more information.

South Whidbey Island State Park

sitka spruce

Three trails here show you a rare sight: a virgin forest bordering Puget Sound. The Forest Discovery Trail is a loop from the first parking lot to the second. Pick up a sketch map at either trailhead or at the ranger's office. This trail offers great views of the sound to the west and of mighty Douglas-fir, grand fir, western redcedar, and western hemlock in the forest. Variety is the highlight of this walk. You will see everything from a cedar swamp to licorice fern to Sitka spruce.

The Beach Trail descends to the beach from the main parking lot, leading you through salmonberry, elderberry, blackberry, bigleaf maple trees, and alder as well as large conifers. The Hobbit Trail, starting near campsite 23, is equally interesting. Both the Hobbit and Beach Trails have steep steps down the bluff. Walking along the beach allows you to make a loop trip of these two trails.

Another trail, the Wilbert Trail, starts across the road from the park entrance and goes into the Classic U Forest. The trail is named for Harry Wilbert, one of the leaders of the citizens' group who built the trail. It's another easy walk through very old Douglas-fir and western redcedar.

The citizens of Whidbey Island came to the rescue of a portion of this forest in 1978 when it was threatened with clearcutting. The state Department of Natural Resources planned to cut the timber for revenue. Whidbey Island residents took the department to court and won. The State Parks Commission bought the land to protect the old growth and add it to the park.

Getting There: Going north on Highway 525 from the ferry terminal at Clinton on Whidbey Island, turn left on Bush Point Road (north of Freeland). Bush Point Road becomes Smugglers Cove Road and takes you to the entrance of South Whidbey Island State Park on the left. Drive past the ranger station and turn right and then left into the paved parking lot. A 7-foot-diameter Douglas-fir with burn scars on its bark greets you in the parking lot. Contact the Washington State Parks and Recreation Commission for more information.

Deception Pass State Park

vagrant shrew

The Hoypus Point Trail on Coronet Bay is an easy walk through a small stand of western hemlock, western redcedar, and very large Douglas-fir. Several side trails invite exploration. Beautiful views of Mount Baker and the Cascades appear as you leave the old growth. Be on the lookout for bald eagles, woodpeckers, and deer.

Look closely at the undergrowth in the forest—notice the mosses, ferns, salal, Oregon-grape, and salmonberry, and the mushrooms that appear unexpectedly. A rich diversity of plant life awaits you in other areas of the park as well, from cranberries and Labrador tea to dune grass and sand verbena.

The park has plenty of recreational opportunities: fishing, boating, swimming, hiking, bicycling, scuba diving, bird-watching, and picnicking. More than 18 miles of trails run throughout the park, and there are plenty of campsites.

Deception Pass gets its name from Captain George Vancouver's confusion. Vancouver first named what he thought was an inlet, Port Gardner. When he discovered that the inlet was really a narrow passage between two islands, he renamed it Deception Pass.

⬥ *Getting There:* From Anacortes, head south on Highway 20 for about 9 miles and cross the high bridge over Deception Pass. Turn east onto Coronet Bay Road (south of the south entrance to Deception Pass State Park). Continue on Coronet Bay Road for about 1 mile past the marina and picnic area to a turnout on the right side of the road. The trail begins at the white gate beside the long wooden fence. This site is about a two-and-a-half-hour drive from Seattle. Contact the Washington State Parks and Recreation Commission for more information.

Charlie Raines

EASTERN CASCADES

🌲 SILVER CREEK 🌲 BUMPING LAKE 🌲 NORTH FORK ENTIAT
RIVER 🌲 WEST FORK TEANAWAY RIVER 🌲 LOST RIVER

The eastern slopes of the Cascades have their own version of ancient forest. Because of the "rainshadow" effects of the mountain range, far less moisture falls here than in western Washington. The type of forest changes, eventually petering out into grassy ridges overlooking the Columbia River to the east. Some of the best old growth used to be found in the valley bottoms, many of which were homesteaded in the nineteenth century or logged in the twentieth century.

Because of the complex effects of weather and topography, the eastside has a far greater diversity of tree species than is found west of the Cascade Crest. In some valleys you can see a dozen types of conifer, including cedar, fir, pine, spruce, and larch.

Fire, a natural part of the ecological cycle, actually creates ideal conditions for some old-growth species such as ponderosa pine. Numerous small fires burn the brush on the forest floor, creating grassy, parklike groves where these trees can flourish. Once tall enough, their thick bark and branchless lower trunks protect them from flames. Unfortunately, the misguided fire suppression approach of Smokey the Bear has worsened the fire risk. Logging the big trees, then replanting with thin-barked firs which are permitted to grow thickly, allows groundfires to race up these "fire ladders" into the crowns of the ponderosas, killing them.

Silver Creek

*northern
flying squirrel*

This trail skirts the side of Silver Creek Canyon leading into a hanging valley—a relic of glacial times—with large Douglas-fir and cedar trees crowding the creek banks. Chickadees, kinglets, and nuthatches flit through the forest. Red crossbills pick seeds out of cones on the tops of firs, and Steller's jays call noisily. You might find a Townsend's solitaire sitting quietly atop a snag. This is also a great place to see signs of elk. There are good campsites along the most forested part of the creek, 2 to 4 miles up.

The lower valley is an old burn, with young grand fir and occasional Douglas-fir snags and large (live) ponderosa pine. The middle (hanging) valley has a variety of old-growth forest types. At about a mile, six large sentinel trees about 3 feet in diameter guard the trail's entrance to the hanging valley. Nearby, a lone yew tree grows gnarly on the side of the trail. A little farther, more large Douglas-fir, hemlock, and cedar tower over a waterfall. A wide, wet flat opens up with a variety of trees: silver fir, subalpine fir, and even cottonwoods, lodgepole, and an occasional white pine. Numerous snags provide habitat for a variety of animals.

Silver Creek is part of the neglected but still relatively intact Kachess Ridge Roadless Area. A checkerboard ownership pattern is increasingly leading to dismemberment of the roadless area as Plum Creek Timber Company logs its railroad grant lands, though not at a square mile at a time, as was the previous practice. Already, many miles of once lonesome trail have been bulldozed by road construction crews. Part of the valley has been purchased with federal funds, through the Land and Water Conservation Fund. However, the purchase of these Plum Creek lands is in doubt, as Congress has nearly eliminated funding for this program. The valley would be off-limits to logging under the Northwest Forest Plan if these lands are acquired by the Forest Service.

⚑ *Getting There:* Though the trailhead is only 1.5 miles from an I-90 interchange, a maze of old logging roads and a dearth of signs can prove confusing. Take the Lake Easton State Park exit (70) off I-90 and drive over the highway to the north side. Turn left onto Sparks Road and follow signs towards Lake Kachess Dam. After 0.5 mile take a right onto Forest Road 4818, and after a further 0.4 mile turn right again onto the dirt road (#203) under the powerlines. At the next junction (0.7 mile) stay left to reach the parking area for trail #1315. You will notice the recent logging activity by Plum Creek Timber Company. Contact the Cle Elum Ranger District for more information.

Bumping Lake

lodgepole pine

The Bumping River Valley is surrounded by the William O. Douglas Wilderness, named after the Supreme Court Justice who hiked there as a boy and later built a cabin at Goose Prairie. Unfortunately, the four old-growth groves described below are not in the wilderness. While these groves are

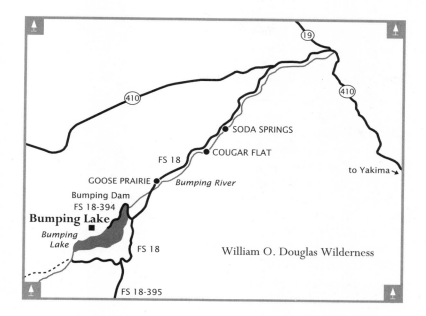

currently protected by the Forest Service, they could be inundated if Bumping Lake is enlarged by the federal Reclamation Service. The dam, built in 1910 by enlarging a natural lake, was rebuilt in 1995.

Huge old Douglas-firs tower above the lake, some with an "eastside" drier pine flavor, others with a "westside" moister feel. The trail is great for kids as it is nearly flat. It is not crowded, although you may share the trail with horses on the steeper Swamp Creek Trail.

The trail (#971) generally parallels the shore. It crosses several talus slopes and dry but diverse forests of grand fir, white pine, lodge-pole pine, and western larch, with the occasional large Douglas-fir. At about 1 mile, below a talus slope, is the first of three groves of giant Douglas-firs. There are several 3 to 4 feet in diameter, with one fire-scarred giant with a nearly 6-foot diameter. Among these ancients are large—but centuries younger—grand fir, hemlock, and spruce, as well as snags and rotting logs.

The second grove, near the lake, has 4-foot diameter Douglas-firs along with large silver firs. The forest appears moister than the earlier dry, rocky slopes. Just a few minutes up the trail the third and grandest grove towers above the trail. First, a huge Douglas-fir over 8 feet in diameter stands on the left side of the trail. A few strides farther, three giant Douglas-firs about 6 feet in diameter, plus two snags of similar size, stand in a circle. Attending these royalty are several other firs too big to get your arms around.

Keep going a few minutes along the trail to see huge anthills in a younger forest. Scattered among them are Douglas-firs 5 to 8 feet in diameter, remnants of a pre-fire forest. As the trail begins to climb, the forest changes as you pass cedar, hemlock, and an occasional white pine.

At the junction with the Swamp Lake Trail (#970) you can drop to Bumping River. You must ford the river carefully as the smooth rocky ledges can be slippery, but the water is less than a foot deep in late summer. A short climb brings you to an overlook where you can see Bridal Veil Falls—actually a cascade over rock. You reach the Swamp Lake trailhead and camping area at just short of 5 miles.

🔺 *Getting There:* From Yakima take US 12 northbound to Highway 410 (Chinook Pass Highway). Follow Highway 410 until about milepost 88. Then turn left onto the paved Bumping River Road (Forest Service [FS] 18, which is also Country Road 2000). Pass the village of Goose Prairie and continue to the Bumping Dam (about 11 miles), where the pavement ends. From this point you can choose which direction to start your hike. Turn right and cross the dam and spillway (FS 18-394). Continue on the dirt road as it follows the north side of Bumping Lake. After passing several cabins, you reach the end of the road (2 miles from the dam). To go clockwise, drive from the dam to the Swamp Lake Trailhead 3.5 miles along the main road and take the right fork at the Deep Creek Road (FS 1800) junction. Contact the Naches Ranger District for more information.

North Fork Entiat River

ponderosa pine cone

The North Fork Entiat River is the main stream of a magnificent 18,000-acre valley still not protected as wilderness. This valley is just one part of the state's largest remaining contiguous roadless area—nearly 150,000 acres in extent. The forest contrasts with the burned and logged hillsides downvalley.

The first few miles of the North Fork Trail (#1437) are an easy walk through alternating groves of old-growth Douglas-fir, lodgepole pine, and some thriving western white pine trees over 2 feet in diameter. These trees have survived the diseases that wiped out their species in most other places (although recently some additional rust infection has been noted). Later on, the trail winds through pretty aspen groves and meadows with fine flowers early in the season. You will find several nice campsites along the bubbling river. Until President Clinton's forest plan, the first couple of miles of trail and much of nearby Duncan Hill and Sheep and Butte Creeks were at risk from timber sales on the shelf at the local ranger station. The area was closed to motorbikes during the Forest Plan fight in 1989.

⚑ **Getting There:** From the village of Entiat on Highway 97, take the Entiat River Road west for 32 miles. Turn right at a fork onto Forest Service Road 5606, and go another 4 miles to the trailhead. Contact the Entiat Ranger District for more information.

pacific jumping mouse

West Fork Teanaway River

The West Fork Teanaway is a secluded valley just north of Cle Elum. While it may not have the biggest trees, it has great diversity.

From the top of the valley, a 1-mile hike brings you to a grove of huge, old cedars. Along the way see the large white pines. A few hemlock indicate the upper valley has something of a "westside" climate, mostly due to significant precipitation and the shading of a mature forest. This could change as Plum Creek Timber Company continues to clearcut in the valley. Although it is within the protective Teanaway Recreation Area, the private lands are not affected by the protection. Plum Creek's new habitat conservation plan would allow this clearcutting to continue. The only answer is acquisition by the Forest Service. For now, look closely for evidence of goshawks and spotted owls.

The lower end of the valley, reached from the Teanaway River Road, is a much drier forest dominated by ponderosa pine and basalt gorges. Once a rich spawning area for salmon, the water diversions for irrigation downstream have nearly eliminated this run. Be prepared to ford the river a couple of times.

⚑ **Getting There:** From Cle Elum, go north on Highway 903 to Roslyn and Ronald, then follow Salmon La Sac Road along the eastern shore of

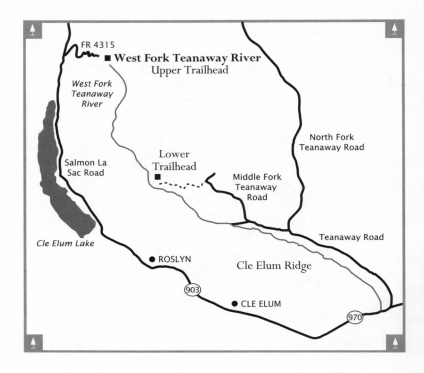

Cle Elum Lake for about 14 miles. Just after the Cooper River Road intersection, turn right onto Forest Service Road 4315, which switch-backs up the ridge. Veer right and follow the new logging road into the upper basin. At the end of the road (southwest corner of section 23), a little exploring may be necessary to find the frayed end of this once remote trail. The lower end of the trail can be reached by going north on Teanaway River Road (off Highway 970 east of Cle Elum), turning right onto Middle Fork Teanaway Road, and following it to the trailhead. Note that the roads here are not very clearly signed. Take along a good map. Contact the Cle Elum Ranger District for more information.

Lost River

The Lost River has some of the finest ancient forest in the Okanogan National Forest. Luckily enough, it also has an easy hiking trail. Pick an early or late summer day to stroll through groves of unbelievably huge ponderosa pine trees

ponderosa pine

and sniff their vanilla-scented bark. Or wander along the banks of the winding river and marvel at this magnificent gateway to the Pasayten Wilderness beyond. Lost River was excluded from the wilderness because of its big trees, many of which were almost logged several years ago (some are still striped with fading blue paint). Spotted owls nesting in the valley saved these great trees. This valley is now in a Late-Successional Reserve so is relatively safe from logging.

The forest here is lush and diverse, including now-rare western white pine as well as redcedar and Douglas-fir. It is home to beavers, mule deer, many types of woodpeckers, and mountain goats. The occasional grizzly bear may come by to scoop salmon from the Lost River. Many campsites are possible on sandbars in the first 4 miles.

⚠ *Getting There:* Drive State Highway 20 to the hamlet of Mazama (1.5 miles east of Early Winters Campground) and turn north off the highway, crossing the Methow River. Turn left after the crossing, onto the Harts Pass Road (Forest Service Road 5400). The trailhead is 0.25 mile after the Lost River bridge, 7.5 miles upstream from Mazama. Contact the Methow Valley Ranger District for more information.

THE FUTURE OF ANCIENT FORESTS

Walking through an ancient forest is a humbling experience. Among the majestic giants is a way of life, an ecosystem that has evolved and thrived for a hundred centuries.

Today all we have left is a fragmented sample of the magnificent forest that once carpeted the Northwest. From these few fragments we gather not only the knowledge of our history, but also keys to our future—new foods and medicines, clean air and water.

Seemingly strong and timeless, yet so threatened, the few remaining stands of old-growth forest are at our mercy. What a shame it would be to have only pictures someday.

The future of most of the remaining old-growth stands lies in the decisions being made by the Forest Service and elected officials. If you are concerned about the future of your favorite segment of ancient forest, or about old growth in general, take its future into your own hands.

Ways to Help

🌲 Introduce the ancient trees to your friends nationwide so that more people will appreciate their special place in our heritage.

🌲 Join one or more of the organizations working to save the Northwest's ancient forests, such as The Wilderness Society, the Northwest Ecosystem Alliance, the Sierra Club, the Washington Environmental Council, or The Mountaineers (see "Who to Contact" at the back of this book).

🌲 Write to the Forest Service to let them know your opinion of the value of old-growth forests and, in particular, describe the stands you know and love.

🌲 When you visit the old trees, stop in at the Ranger District office and let the staff know your concerns.

🌲 Tell your Senators and Representative what you think about ancient forests. Ask that decisions about federal forest management policies reflect the importance of protecting our groves of old trees. Local leaders need to hear from you too.

♠ Write letters to the editors of your local newspapers and to the editorial boards of your TV and radio stations.

♠ Most important, as you grow weary of the bureaucratic maneuvering necessary to protect our forests, take a break. Go back to the woods. Listen to the silence. Breathe deep of the scented air. Stretch your legs where the ground is covered with needles. Stretch your neck to see the tops of giant trees. Look, listen, smell, feel—and experience renewal from the ancient places.

MORE ANCIENT FOREST AREAS

ncient forests can be visited in a number of other places, some of which are listed below. Call the appropriate ranger station or national park (see "Who to Contact") for more information. Numerous excellent hiking books (see "Suggested Reading") and maps are available at bookstores and outdoor equipment stores.

OLYMPIC PENINSULA

Gray Wolf River. A small spectacular stand in a fire-scarred mosaic. Located in the northeast portion of the Olympic National Forest and Park near Sequim, partly protected in the Buckhorn Wilderness.

Lower Big Quilcene River Trail. In an area of many clearcuts and second growth, there are gorgeous ancient trees between the trail and the river before the first river crossing.

Duckabush River. A strenuous hike. The old growth is before the Big Hump area.

Upper South Fork Skokomish. A splendid example of an ancient forest. Large old Douglas-fir, silver fir, western hemlock, and redcedar along the river in the southeast portion of the Olympics. Access road is closed until April 30.

Maple Glade Nature Trail. New trail (1988) on the north side of Lake Quinault. Visit the Quinault Ranger Station for information.

Queets Rain Forest. You must ford a dangerous, fast-flowing river to get to the trailhead and to the miles of rain forest.

Rugged Ridge Trail. High-elevation hemlock and silver fir grow on a short steep trail adjacent to the Olympic National Park boundary.

Marymere Falls Trail. In the Lake Crescent area. Find the grand fir, the self-guided Nature Trail, and the 90-foot-high falls.

Northern Cascades

Damfino Creek. A high alpine summer hiking opportunity in a very important wildlife habitat area east of Bellingham and just south of the Canadian border. Use Trail #688 (Boundary Way), which is forested for a mile or so before breaking out into high huckleberry country.

Diobsud Creek. A very accessible flat trail above a narrow ravine (700 to 900 feet in elevation) in an old-growth forest. Many snag-dwelling birds live here. A good fishing spot. About 4 miles north of Marblemount. Use Forest Service (FS) Road 1050 to get to Trail #631.

Noisy Creek. You need a boat to cross from the north shore of Baker Lake to Trail #609 for a very rewarding hike in the ancient forest. The boat and motor can be rented for a day from the Baker Lake Lodge. Call (206) 853-8325 for information.

Baker Lake Nature Trail. A self-guided trail and a good introduction to old growth in a small area west of Baker Lake on FS 11 near Rocky Creek.

Baker River Trail #606. "Luxurious rain forest." Check on trail conditions.

Kindy Creek. A real cathedral forest between Cascade River and protected Glacier Peak Wilderness. The old growth is next to the trail. Use FS 1570 from 2 miles east of Mineral Park picnic area.

Big Beaver Valley. In the Ross Lake National Recreational Area of the North Cascades National Park Complex. Enormous cedar, Douglas-fir, hemlock, and ghostly silver fir thrive here. Take Highway 20 to Ross Lake Resort and use the Beaver Loop Trail.

Mount Higgins to Myrtle Lake Area. Cedar can be viewed to the north from Highway 530 about 17 miles east of Arlington. Land closest to river is private, but the slopes are Forest Service land. The lower end of the trail is on Department of Natural Resources (DNR) land, which was harvested recently.

Barlow Pass. A 1-mile switchback trail through an ancient forest leads to a magnificent view. Use Barlow Point Trail #709.

Heather Lake. Hike through regrowing clearcuts and enter a cathedral forest with behemoth cedar. The trail climbs to subalpine forest and meadow in a valley close to Mount Pilchuck. The trailhead is 1 mile east of Verlot.

Lake 22. This popular Research Natural Area was set aside in 1947 for study of water, wildlife, and timber in a virgin state. Giant cedar and a series of waterfalls highlight this area. Use Trail #702. Lake 22 is located 2 miles east of Verlot Public Service Center.

Blanca Lake. There are a lot of spectacular old trees along a steep trail, with some Douglas-firs 8 feet in diameter. The first 3 miles are outside the wilderness and thus unprotected. Blanca Lake is located northeast of Index off FS 63. Use Trail #1052.

Barclay Lake. This is a low-elevation area at the base of Baring Mountain, about 6 miles east of Index off Highway 2. Use Trail #1055 (a short trail).

Miller River. Huge cedar, hemlock, and Douglas-fir grow in a spectacular deep valley. Drive about 10 miles east of Index off Highway 2 to FS 6410.

Deception Creek. This is a fine example of mid-elevation old growth. The trail takes you into the Alpine Lakes Wilderness through virgin forest and by a special creek. Approximately 8 miles east of Skykomish. Use Trail #1059.

North Fork Skykomish. Can be viewed from a car on either side of the road after passing Troublesome Creek Campground. (See West Cady Creek in the Northern Cascades section.)

Surprise Creek. Gorgeous large cedar are along the first mile of trail outside the wilderness area. Great waterfalls. Use Trail #1060, which enters Alpine Lakes Wilderness. About 10 miles east of Skykomish.

CENTRAL CASCADES

Sunday Creek. Northeast of North Bend. The trail meanders along the south side of North Fork Snoqualmie River valley among giant cedar and into the Alpine Lakes Wilderness.

Pratt River. You need a boat to cross the river but once across you will find a magnificent forest. Partially logged early in the century, survivors included Douglas-fir up to 9 feet in diameter. There have been conflicts between mountain bikers and hikers in this area.

Hester Lake. Trail #1105, a steep trail into the Alpine Lakes Wilderness, takes you into virgin forests northeast of North Bend.

Mount Phelps. North Bend area. The last contiguous old growth in the North Fork Snoqualmie drainage. Take the North Fork Snoqualmie Road to the Lenox Creek crossing.

Clearwater Wilderness. See huge cedar, fir, and hemlock complete with hanging moss. Near the Carbon River entrance of Mount Rainier National Park. Use Trails #1176, #1177, and #1178.

Lost Creek/Huckleberry Creek. A lovely and critical old growth site at the creeks' confluence just north of Mount Rainier National Park. Take Highway 410 to FS 73. Use Trail #1182.

Moss Lake Nature Trail. A great example of a cedar swamp. (See Camp Sheppard–Snoquera Falls directions in "Central Cascades.")

Goat Creek. Located off FS 7174 and near Crystal Mountain, a short trail meanders along Goat Creek in a setting of ancient trees.

SOUTHERN CASCADES

Dry Creek. Mountain goats use this old growth for thermal cover. The area is in a hanging valley and is untouched. About 3 miles southwest of Packwood take FS 20, then FS 2010 to its end; cross country (at your own risk) into the drainage (Trail #125 nearby). The lower trailhead is on DNR land; a small salvage parcel has been logged but the sale boundary never crosses the trail.

High Rock. Lovely forests and superb views of Mount Rainier from the High Rock Lookout (one of three remaining fire lookouts in the area). Northwest of Randle, turn south off Highway 706 onto FS 52 about 3 miles west of the Nisqually entrance to Mount Rainier National Park. After 3 miles turn on FS 84 and go 10 miles to trailhead at Towhead Gap. Explore a network of Forest Service roads and trails, such as Teeley Creek Trail #251.

Johnson Creek Area. A bushwhack scramble along the creek bed— for the hardy and experienced. Southeast of Packwood along FS 21. Best old growth is between Glacier Creek and Deception Creek junction. Get a topographic map to show the lay of the land.

Boundary Trail #1 near Elk Pass. Pumice from Mount St. Helens lightens the forest and softens the trail. Great huckleberries in season. About 32 miles south of Randle on FS 25, or 22 miles north of the junction of FS 25 and FS 90 (near the Pine Creek Information Center).

Quartz Creek Big Trees Botanical Area. Combine visiting this 60-acre site with a trip to Mount St. Helens. About 18 miles south of Randle. Take FS 25, then FS 26 across the Cispus River to FS 2608.

Buck Creek. Wildflowers along with large trees. North of Trout Lake on FS 23 toward Mount Adams, then take FS 80, then FS 031. Use Trail #54.

Soda Peaks Trail. Fortunately this area has been preserved in the Trapper Creek Wilderness. The entire Trail #133 goes through an ancient forest. Stiff climb from Government Springs or a short hike from FS 54.

Falls Creek Trail (# 152). Climbs through 2 miles of beautiful old-growth forest to the top of a three-stage waterfall, while trail #152A follows the creek 1.5 miles through old-growth Douglas-fir to the base of the falls. From Carson (38 miles east of Vancouver) take Wind River Highway north to FS 30 and then right on FS 3062 to trailheads.

EASTERN CASCADES

Barton Creek. On the east side of Bumping Lake. This forest looks like it belongs west of the Cascades: it is wet and has large hemlock, cedar, and fir. A dirt road (FS 665) leads east from the dam about 0.25 mile. The trail is actually an old miners' road and is not signed or maintained.

Heather Lake. Up the Little Wenatchee River is a forest of westside fir and hemlock. The trail (#1526) starts in a clearcut, passes through an old burn, and then enters the ancient forests. In places you can find ash on the ground. Beyond the big trees is the wilderness boundary and the usual destination is Heather Lake.

Mad River. Ponderosa pine and other conifers up to 3 feet in diameter hug the steep valley walls. Unfortunately, the Mad River Trail is in bad shape due to 1994 fires, with bridges burned out.

South Fork Taneum Creek. Several spotted owls nest in this valley, using thick branches called "witches brooms," caused by a plant parasite. Plum Creek Timber Company has plans for more roads and logging.

Mineral Creek. Above Kachess Lake adjacent to Alpine Lakes Wilderness. Plum Creek did some helicopter logging in 1995 above the trail.

Scatter Creek. A network of trails threads this Upper Cle Elum River valley adjacent to Alpine Lakes Wilderness. Plum Creek could log this at any time.

Chewuch River. There is a surprising amount of ancient forest along the Chewuch River Road (FS 51). Most are upstream of Chris Creek, but below there are large ponderosa pine selectively logged numerous times over the past fifty years. Past Andrews Creek, there are several groves of old growth.

Farewell Creek. Mature ponderosa pine (up to 2 feet in diameter) grow along the first 2 miles of trail, just off the Chewuch River Road.

Little Bridge Creek. The west fork of this creek (tributary of the Twisp River) has Douglas-fir up to 4 feet in diameter and some ponderosa pine. Start on Highway 403, then take Road #4415. (The official trail is up North Fork but you will not see as interesting old growth from there.)

WHO TO CONTACT

T he following addresses and telephone numbers will be useful as you seek out the ancient forests described in this book. Remember always to call the ranger district or national park before heading out to check on road and traffic conditions.

ENVIRONMENTAL ORGANIZATIONS

The Wilderness Society
900 17th Street NW
Washington, DC 20006
(202) 824-3400

The Wilderness Society Northwest Office
1424 Fourth Avenue #816
Seattle, WA 98101
(206) 624-6430

Sierra Club Cascade Chapter
8511 - 15th Avenue NE
Seattle, WA 98115
(206) 523-2147

Washington Wilderness Coalition
4516 Sunnyside N
Seattle, WA 98103
(206) 633-1992

Washington Environmental Council
1100 Second Avenue #102
Seattle, WA 98101
(206) 622-8103

Western Ancient Forest Campaign
1101 14th Street NW #140
Washington, DC 20005
(202) 789-2844

The Mountaineers
300 Third Avenue West
Seattle, WA 98119
(206) 284-6310

GENERAL INFORMATION

National Park Service, Northwest Regional Office
83 South King Street, Suite 212
Seattle, WA 98104
(206) 553-5622

Outdoor Recreation Information Center
915 Second Avenue, Suite 442, Federal Building
Seattle, WA 98174
(206) 220-7450

Washington State Parks and Recreation Commission
Public Affairs Office/Park Information
7150 Cleanwater Lane, KY-11
Olympia, WA 98504
(360) 902-8563

OLYMPIC PENINSULA

Olympic National Park
600 East Park Avenue
Port Angeles, WA 98362
(360) 452-4501 or (360) 452-0329 (recorded message)

Olympic National Forest
1835 Black Lake Boulevard SW
Olympia, WA 98502
(360) 956-2400

Quilcene Ranger Station
P.O. Box 280
Quilcene, WA 98376
(360) 765-3368

Quinault Ranger Station
P.O. Box 9
Quinault, WA 98575
(360) 288-2525

Hoodsport Ranger Station
P.O. Box 68
Hoodsport, WA 98548
(360) 877-5254
Sol Duc Ranger Station
Route 1, Box 5750, Hwy 101
Forks, WA 98331
(360) 374-6522

NORTHERN CASCADES
North Cascades National Park System Complex
2015 Highway 20
Sedro Wooley, WA 98284
(360) 856-5700
Mount Baker/Snoqualmie National Forest
21905 - 64th Avenue West
Mountlake Terrace, WA 98043
(206) 775-9702
Mount Baker Ranger District
2105 Highway 20
Sedro Wooley, WA 98284
(206) 677-5700
Darrington Ranger District
1405 Emmens Street
Darrington, WA 98241
(206) 436-1155
Verlot Public Service Center
33515 Mountain Loop Highway
Granite Falls, WA 98252
(360) 691-7791
North Bend Ranger District
42404 SE North Bend Way
North Bend, WA 98045
(360) 888-1321
Skykomish Ranger District
P.O. Box 305
Skykomish, WA 98288
(360) 677-2414

CENTRAL CASCADES

Mount Rainier National Park
Tahoma Woods, Star Route
Ashford, WA 98304
(360) 569-2211

Federation Forest State Park
49201 (Highway 410) Chinook Pass Road
Enumclaw, WA 98022
(206) 663-2207

White River Ranger District
857 Roosevelt Avenue East
Enumclaw, WA 98022
(206) 825-6585

SOUTHERN CASCADES

Gifford Pinchot National Forest
6926 East Fourth Plain Boulevard
Vancouver, WA 98668
(360) 750-5001

Mount Adams Ranger District
2455 Highway 141
Trout Lake, WA 98650
(509) 395-3400

Mount St. Helens National Volcanic Monument
42218 NE Yale Bridge Road
Amboy, WA 98601
(360) 247-5473

Randle Ranger District
10024 U.S. Highway 12
Randle, WA 98377
(360) 497-7565

Packwood Ranger District
13068 U.S. Highway 12
Packwood, WA 98361
(360) 494-5515

Wind River Ranger District
 MP 1.23 Hemlock Road
 Carson, WA 98610
 (509) 427-3200

EASTERN CASCADES
Wenatchee National Forest
 P.O. Box 811, 215 Melody Lane
 Wenatchee, WA 98807-0811
 (509) 662-4335
Cle Elum Ranger District
 803 West 2nd Street
 Cle Elum, WA 98922
 (509) 674-4411
Naches Ranger District
 10061 Highway 12
 Naches, WA 98937
 (509) 653-2205
Entiat Ranger District
 P.O. Box 476, 2108 Entiat Way
 Entiat, WA 98822
 (509) 784-1511
Okanogan National Forest
 1241 - 2nd Avenue South
 Okanogan, WA 98840
 (509) 826-3275
Methow Valley Ranger District
 Winthrop Office, P.O. Box 579
 Winthrop, WA 98862
 (509) 996-2266
Methow Valley Ranger District
 Twisp Office, P.O. Box 188
 Twisp, WA 98856
 (509) 997-2131

SUGGESTED READING

Arno, Stephen F., and Ramona P. Hammerly. *Northwest Trees*. Seattle: The Mountaineers, 1977.

Burton, Joan. *Best Hikes with Children in Western Washington and the Cascades*. 2 vols. Seattle: The Mountaineers, 1988.

Cissel, John, and Diane Cissel. *50 Old Growth Hikes in the Southern Washington Cascades*. Map. Portland: Old-Growth Day Hikes, 1996.

Dietrich, Bill. *The Final Forest: The Battle for the Last Great Trees of the Pacific Northwest*. New York: Simon & Schuster, 1992.

Durbin, Kathie. *Tree Huggers: Victory, Defeat, and Renewal in the Pacific Northwest Ancient Forests Campaign*. Seattle: The Mountaineers, 1996.

Kelly, David, and Gary Braasch. *Secrets of the Old Growth Forest*. Salt Lake City: Peregrine Smith Books, 1988.

Kirk, Ruth, and Charles Mauzy, eds. *The Enduring Forests: Northern California, Oregon, Washington, British Columbia, and Southeast Alaska*. Seattle: The Mountaineers, 1996.

Manning, Harvey, and Peggy Manning. *Walks and Hikes in the Foothills and Lowlands around Puget Sound*. Seattle: The Mountaineers, 1995.

Maser, Chris. *The Redesigned Forest*. San Pedro: R&E Miles, 1988.

Maser, Chris. *Forest Primeval*. San Francisco: Sierra Club Books, 1989.

Morrison, Peter. *Old Growth in the Pacific Northwest, A Status Report*. Washington, DC: The Wilderness Society, 1988.

Mueller, Marge, and Ted Mueller. *Exploring Washington's Wild Areas: A Guide for Hikers, Backpackers, Climbers, X-C Skiers, and Paddlers*. Seattle: The Mountaineers, 1994.

Norse, Elliott. *Ancient Forests of the Pacific Northwest*. Washington, DC: Island Press, 1990.

Olson, Jeffrey. *Pacific Northwest Lumber and Wood Products: An Industry in Transition, National Forests Policies for the Future, Volume 4*. Washington, DC: The Wilderness Society and National Wildlife Federation, 1988.

Spring, Ira, and Harvey Manning. *50 Hikes in Mount Rainier National Park*. 3d ed. Seattle: The Mountaineers, 1988.

Spring, Vicky, Ira Spring, and Harvey Manning. *100 Hikes in Washington's Alpine Lakes*. 2d ed. Seattle: The Mountaineers, 1993.

Spring, Ira, and Harvey Manning. *100 Hikes in the South Cascades and Olympics*. 2d ed. Seattle: The Mountaineers, 1992.

Spring, Ira, and Harvey Manning. *100 Hikes in Washington's North Cascades National Park Region*. 2d ed. Seattle: The Mountaineers, 1994.

Spring, Ira, and Harvey Manning. *100 Hikes in Washington's Glacier Peak Region: The North Cascades*. 2d ed. Seattle: The Mountaineers, 1996.

Whitney, Stephen R. *Nature Walks In & Around Seattle*. Seattle: The Mountaineers, 1987.

The Wilderness Society. *End of the Ancient Forests*. Washington, DC: The Wilderness Society, 1988.

Tim Crosby

ACKNOWLEDGMENTS

This book was first published in 1989 by The Wilderness Society as *Visitors' Guide to Ancient Forests in Western Washington*. This new edition published by The Mountaineers has been expanded to include information about ancient forests east of the Cascade Crest. The new section on the Eastern Cascades was written by Charlie Raines.

The Dittmar family, authors of the first, original section of this book, wish to thank the following friends and relatives who contributed to The Wilderness Society in Stan Dittmar's memory for the publication of the first edition:

The contribution in memory of Joe and Nell Wilburn, and Donna, Meagan, and Mark McDonald.

Jon Gardescu for his illustrations.

Mark Lawler, Rick McGuire, Tim McNulty, Bob Pearson, Charlie Raines, Susan Saul, and the many other volunteer leaders in the conservation movement in Western Washington who know these forests intimately and contributed generously of their time, knowledge, and advice.

David Guren, Mary Darlington, Mark Winey, Susan Olson, and many others who scouted the numerous areas and gave us valuable information or assisted us in other ways.

The staffs in national, state, and city parks and Forest Service ranger districts for valuable information and directions.

The photographers who loaned us their beautiful prints.

The Wilderness Society staff for their assistance in creating the guide.

The Mountaineers Books offers special thanks to Matt Golec, Conservation Associate at The Mountaineers Club, who contributed generously of his time and expertise to revise and update this second edition.

THE WILDERNESS SOCIETY was founded in 1935 by a group of ecologists "distressed by the exceedingly swift passing of wilderness in a country which recently abounded in the richest and noblest of wilderness forms. . . ." The society purposed to do all they could to safeguard what was left of wild lands, and most of its first thirty years were spent building support for and eventually gaining passage of the Wilderness Act of 1964. Since then, over 100 million acres of wilderness have been protected in the United States, including more than 4 million acres in Washington State.

The organization's central ethic, as articulated by co-founder Aldo Leopold, is the conviction that the land is not a commodity to be used but an inheritance to be cherished. In the last two decades, The Wilderness Society's focus has broadened beyond the preservation of wilderness areas to include advocating for sustainable management of land and resources, including commodity uses and multiple-use lands. This has put the organization squarely in the middle of high-profile political debates over the fate of the nation's prime forests, parks, refuges, and rangelands. The group's work is accomplished by its network of nine regional offices, including the Northwest Regional Office in Seattle.

THE MOUNTAINEERS, founded in 1906, is a nonprofit outdoor activity and conservation club, whose mission is "to explore, study, preserve, and enjoy the natural beauty of the outdoors. . . ." Based in Seattle, Washington, the club is now the third-largest such organization in the United States, with 15,000 members and five branches throughout Washington State.

The Mountaineers sponsors both classes and year-round outdoor activities in the Pacific Northwest, which include hiking, mountain climbing, ski-touring, snowshoeing, bicycling, camping, kayaking and canoeing, nature study, sailing, and adventure travel. The club's conservation division supports environmental causes through educational activities, sponsoring legislation, and presenting informational programs. All club activities are led by skilled, experienced volunteers, who are dedicated to promoting safe and responsible enjoyment and preservation of the outdoors.

If you would like to participate in these organized outdoor activities or the club's programs, consider a membership in The Mountaineers. For information and an application, write or call The Mountaineers, Club Headquarters, 300 Third Avenue West, Seattle, Washington 98119; (206) 284-6310; clubmail@mountaineers.org.

The Mountaineers Books, an active, nonprofit publishing program of the club, produces guidebooks, instructional texts, historical works, natural history guides, and works on environmental conservation. All books produced by The Mountaineers are aimed at fulfilling the club's mission.

Send or call for our catalog of more than 300 outdoor titles:

The Mountaineers Books
1001 SW Klickitat Way, Suite 201
Seattle, WA 98134
1-800-553-4453; e-mail: mbooks@mountaineers.org